The Illustrated Military History of Canada

THE WAR OF 1812

THE WAR OF 1812

The War that Both Sides Won

WESLEY B. TURNER

Dundurn Press
Toronto and Oxford
1990

Copyediting: Mark Fenton
Design and Production: JAQ
Printing and Binding: Metropole Litho Inc., Quebec, Canada

The writing of this manuscript and the publication of this book were made possible by support from several sources. The publisher wishes to acknowledge the generous assistance and ongoing support of **The Canada Council, The Book Publishing Industry Development Programme of the Department of Communications,**and **The Ontario Arts Council.**

Care has been taken to trace the ownership of copyright material used in the text (including the illustrations). The author and publisher welcome any information enabling them to rectify any reference or credit in subsequent editions.

J. Kirk Howard, Publisher

First Printing: 1990
Second Printing: 1993

Dundurn Press Limited
2181 Queen Street East
 Suite 301
Toronto, Canada
M4E 1E5

Dundurn Distribution Limited
73 Lime Walk
Headington
Oxford 0X3 7AD
England

Canadian Cataloguing in Publication Data

Turner, Wesley B., 1933-
   The war that both sides won

(The Illustrated military history of Canada)
Includes bibliographical references.
ISBN 1-55002-075-7

1. Canada - History - War of 1812.* 2. United States - History - War of 1812. I. Title.
II. Series.

FC442.T87 1990   971.03'4   C90-095150-8
E359.85.T87 1990

Cover: The British capture of the *Somers* and the *Ohio* in the Niagara River, off Fort Erie (Ontario), August 12 1814. (Watercolour and gouache by Owen Staples. Courtesy of the Toronto Metropolitan Library.)

To my wife, Diane

CONTENTS

ACKNOWLEDGMENTS

The writing of this book has benefitted enormously from the critical reading and constructive comments of my colleague R.G. Phillips. I want to thank Shirlee Wallace and Phyllis Riesberry for their patience while typing each successive version. My thanks also to Mary Bell and the staff of the Buffalo and Erie County Historical Society library and archives; Don Lokker, the Niagara Falls Public Library, New York; and Brian Dunnigan and the Old Fort Niagara Association. Finally I would like to thank Kirk Howard and Mark Fenton for their editorial assistance at Dundurn Press.

SURGITE

Sir Isaac Brock.
(Courtesy of Brock University.)

PREFACE

TRAGEDY AND FARCE, bravery and cowardice, intelligence and foolishness, sense and nonsense: these contrasts and more, characterized the War of 1812. The story is interesting in itself. And this interest continues to be renewed by current discoveries which further illuminate the period: for example, the discovery in 1975 and subsequent photographing of the *Hamilton* and *Scourge* on the bottom of Lake Ontario; and the 1987 find of skeletons on the shore of Lake Erie at Snake Hill, grisly casualties of the fighting around Fort Erie in August-September, 1814. As these finds and a constant flow of writings show, the War has exercised an indelible influence on American and Canadian views of themselves and of each other — a further reason for taking yet another look at its course and character.

This book derives from my *The War of 1812, the War for Canada,* written as a school text but which also elicited interest from many quarters and led to requests for copies. The supply of books was never enough to meet these requests and, after the original work went out of print, I decided to revise it for the general reader rather than simply reprint a textbook.

The book was written to provide a succinct yet comprehensive account of the War of 1812 that would both interest and inform the general reader. At the same time, historians may find this a useful, short, up to date version of that formative event. I did not attempt a radical or unusual interpretation. Instead I have included more than a single viewpoint with the intention of providing enjoyment to both American and Canadian readers out of which, perhaps, they may gain some understanding of the important effects this War had on each country.

INTRODUCTION

IN JUNE 1812 the contagion of war spread far beyond the European continent where it had raged for two decades from the early years of the French Revolution. In the United States, President James Madison delivered a war message to Congress on June 1st and, after approval by both Houses, signed a Declaration of War against Great Britain on the 18th. A week later, thousands of kilometres to the east, Emperor Napoleon Bonaparte led the most powerful army in Europe across the Niemen River into Russia. The obvious difference in size and distance does not obscure the connection between these two events. The Napoleonic Wars in Europe not only helped cause war in North America, they would directly affect its entire course. It may be said that the War of 1812 was the North American phase of the Napoleonic Wars.

In an effort to defeat Napoleon, Britain adopted measures that elicited protests from the Americans and contributed significantly to their declaration of war. At first, with its forces tied up fighting the French in the Peninsula (Spain and Portugal), Britain could send little help to its North American colonies. But Napoleon's invasion of Russia turned into a stunning disaster that virtually destroyed his "Grand Army." He raised more troops and fought on, but suffered an increasing number of defeats. The wearing down of the French armies enabled Britain to spare more attention, troops and supplies for North America. Once Napoleon finally surrendered, the United States could no longer hope to win its war against Britain.

One historian has called the War of 1812 the "Incredible War," and there were indeed many incredible aspects to it — including the very fact that it happened. Britain and the United States had more reasons to remain at peace than to fight.

In the summer of 1812 the outcome of such a war seemed obvious to many Americans, Canadians and Britons. There appeared no possibility that Upper Canada could successfully resist

12

American invasion. After its fall, the easy conquest of Lower Canada would follow, although the British might hold on to Quebec City. This anticipated course of the War did not happen. Something else that was unexpected was the success of individual American warships in sea battles with British warships. Surely the oddest aspect is that both sides believe they won the War.

If the beginning and course did not meet expectations, neither did the peace treaty. The Treaty of Ghent ignored most of the reasons that President Madison had given for starting the conflict. It appeared that the treaty did not settle the problems bedeviling Anglo-American relations, yet the basic principles of this agreement of December 1814 have endured to the present.

The Napoleonic Wars in Europe dragged on for years (from 1792 to 1815 with some gaps) and often involved huge armies fighting long battles and suffering terrible losses. By contrast, the War of 1812 lasted two and a half years and was fought by tiny armies and navies in short engagements. Wellington's casualties at Waterloo (15,000) were virtually equal to the total combined casualties suffered by the two sides fighting in North America. Does all this mean that War of 1812 lacks importance and really deserves no more than passing attention? Not at all. The War was brief but its scope was continent-wide for it ranged from the eastern seaboard of the United States to the mouth of the Columbia River on the Pacific coast and from Lake Superior to the Gulf of Mexico. The American Adjutant General later estimated that there had been more than 500,000 enlistments in various American forces during the War, a figure that represented 47% of the white male population between the ages of 16 and 45.[1] This suggests that the experience of enlistment was widespread and affected many families. The War changed the lives of many Canadians and Americans. It significantly influenced the development of each country. That curious little War provides a fundamental reason for Canada's existence as a nation today and still affects what being Canadian means. The United States was perhaps less profoundly affected, but afterwards, there was an increased pride in the nation and a feeling of greater security because both the British and the Indian threats had been eliminated from the northeast.

Finally, the war brought no victory or benefit to the native peoples south and west of Lake Erie. To them this was not a little or insignificant war, but one of survival, and by 1814 they could see that they had lost.

1

BACKGROUND TO WAR, 1802-1812

N APOLEON CREATED A sprawling empire in Europe between 1802 and 1812 through military conquest and alliances. But his ability to extend his power beyond the continent ended in 1805 when Admiral Nelson destroyed the French fleet at the Battle of Trafalgar. From that point on, the Royal Navy stood between Napoleon and invasion across the Channel. He could not assault the fortress of Britain nor could he prevent the British from sending armies to support his enemies on the continent. Napoleon therefore turned to the only weapon left by which he might hope to defeat the "nation of shopkeepers": economic warfare.

In November 1806, Napoleon ordered all European ports under his control closed to British ships. Later he decreed that neutral ships would be seized if they visited a British port before entering a continental port. Britain replied with a series of Orders in Council. These required all neutral ships to enter British ports and obtain a licence before they could sail to Europe. Neutrals had to obey French decrees or British Orders. What choice could a ship's master make? It was Britain that had the seapower to enforce its blockade and require neutral ships to obey its rules. The most important neutral nation trading with Europe was the United States. British interference with American ships would help bring on the War of 1812.

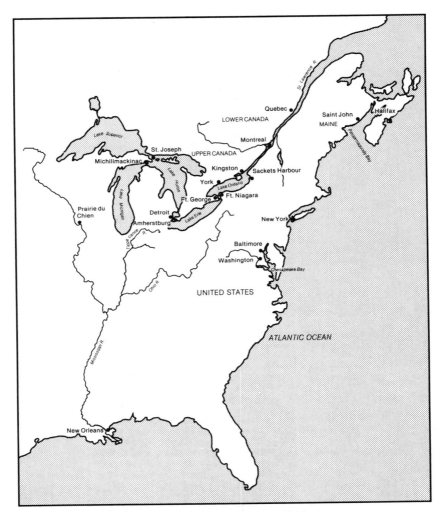

Eastern North America, 1812.
[Reprinted from The War of 1812: The War For Canada, *by W.B. Turner, (Toronto, Grolier Limited, 1982), p. 9.]*

BRITISH NORTH AMERICA AND THE UNITED STATES

On the eve of the war, Britain's North American colonies stretched from the Atlantic Ocean to the western end of Lake Erie and the shores of Lake Huron. Their populations were growing steadily but slowly. Lower Canada (later Quebec province) had about 300,000 people; New Brunswick and Nova Scotia had perhaps 80,000; and estimates for Upper Canada (Ontario) range from 60,000 to 80,000.

The smaller populations of Newfoundland, Prince Edward Island and Cape Breton brought the total to something over half a million. Numbers are only part of the story, for the inhabitants were scattered, living mostly on farms. Towns were small and industries few. These colonies possessed scanty means of making war.

When war threatened, it quickly became clear that Upper Canada was the most vulnerable of the colonies. The biggest problem was transportation. Roads were few and those that did exist were dreadful: deeply rutted sticky mud in the spring thaw and whenever rain fell. Even in dry weather holes, tree stumps, and unbridged rivers discomforted and delayed travellers. Transportation by water was better, but rapids on the St. Lawrence River prevented ships sailing the 300 kilometres from Montreal to Kingston. A few canals had been built around these obstacles, but only small, flat-bottomed boats (bateaux) could navigate through them. At the rapids, goods had to be taken off the boats and carried around. The journey took several days. Travel was easier and faster west of Kingston because ships could sail to York (now Toronto) and Newark (Niagara-on-the-Lake). To go farther required another portage from Queenston up the Niagara River along the Portage Road to Chippawa. Sailing ships could then take people and goods to the few small settlements that dotted Lake Erie's shores.

Upper Canada was too weak to defend itself. Its small population was scattered along the 1,300 kilometres from Cornwall on the St. Lawrence to Amherstburg on Lake Erie. The people did not grow all the food nor did they make all the goods they needed. With their own resources, they could not provide an army or even support British troops. Help from Britain in the form of men, money, supplies, and ships was essential.

All these defence needs depended on a route that the

Americans could easily cut. They had only to march an army north and block the St. Lawrence south of Montreal, and Upper Canada would fall into their hands without their even having to fight there. The British government and the authorities in Canada were always very concerned about the safety of the route from Montreal to Amherstburg.

The United States, with its rapidly growing population of almost 7.5 million was clearly much stronger than Canada. Settlers were filling up New York, Pennsylvania, and Ohio, moving ever closer to the Canadian border. Along the Niagara River, pioneer communities like Buffalo, Black Rock and Lewiston were still small, but they had good roads connecting them with well-populated areas to the east and south. Not far distant were rich farms and expanding cities with factories. The American population could provide thousands of soldiers, and the farms and factories could supply most of their needs. American supply routes ran overland and out of easy range of British forces.

Farther west in Pennsylvania, Ohio and the Michigan Territory, roads were few so that travel was by river or along forest paths. These routes were not only more difficult but also less safe from sudden Indian attack.

INDIANS OF THE NORTHWEST

Indians had been resisting the advance of American settlement in the Old Northwest (south of Lake Erie, north of the Ohio River) since the 1780s. Nonetheless, thousands of Americans moved into the area every year, raising Ohio's population to over 230,000 people and Kentucky's to about 400,000 by 1810. These settlers wanted to drive out the Indians in order to farm the land.

Two Shawnee leaders, Tecumseh and his brother the Prophet (Tenskwatawa), recognized that disunity among the tribes was the principal weakness of their people. They were brave and far-sighted men. In 1805, they began trying to organize a confederacy of all the Indian tribes in the territories threatened by advancing American settlement.

On its own, a tribe could be forced to surrender its lands or be bribed into trading them away. Between 1803 and 1809, Governor William Henry Harrison of the Indiana Territory did this repeatedly with Indians south and west of Lake Erie. Some-

Cartoon depicting British/Indian relations.
[Courtesy of Lilly Library, Indiana University, Bloomington, Indiana.]

times two tribes claimed the same lands and there would be conflict between them. Only by uniting, Tecumseh and the Prophet insisted, could the Indians settle quarrels among themselves and be strong enough to resist American pressure. They urged Indians to rely on their own abilities to create a great Indian nation instead of adopting the white man's ways. But until this could be accomplished, they needed allies and looked for help to the British in Canada. Many Indians had supported the British side in the American Revolution and as an aftermath of that war, some of the Iroquois, the Miamis, the Shawnees and other tribes had been trying to establish an Indian state south and west of Lake Erie. In such a state Indians would control their own lives and land. American settlers would not be able to move in whenever they wanted.

The British government supported this idea of an Indian state because it would provide a buffer for Upper Canada. While few British immigrants were coming to the province, many Americans were. The government feared that if many more moved in, they might become strong enough to pressure the

19

American government into attempting to annex Upper Canada. This danger would be lessened considerably if there were Indian-held territory along the Canadian border.

Fur traders also supported the idea of an Indian state. They wanted to continue trading with the Indians around the Great Lakes and to the west. But the advance of American settlement was steadily (and, as it turned out, permanently) ending the fur trade. The traders and their Indian allies would play an important role in the war to come.

Every year Indians came to Amherstburg, Fort St. Joseph and other British posts to receive presents of food, clothing, guns and ammunition from the British government, distributed through the Indian Department. This department's officers, or agents, met Indians at the posts, visited their villages and sometimes married Indian women. These men thus learned to understand Indians and their feelings. Their services were of great value to the British, for they attended Indian councils to listen and to give advice.

Many Indians, including Tecumseh and the Prophet, did not like their dependence on the British, feeling that it undermined Indian culture and self-respect. But most could not give up the presents they were given because they had no other way to obtain these goods, particularly the weapons they needed to defend their lands against the Americans. Thus, when war came, Tecumseh and his followers felt they had no choice but to support the British. These Indians fought for their survival, not to maintain British rule over Canada.

The Americans viewed British support of the Indians as a threat to their government's policy of trying to force the Indians to give up their hunting lands and become farmers like American settlers. They believed that the British stirred up the Indians to fight and supplied them with weapons for that purpose, endangering thousands of American lives. The British insisted, on the contrary, that they tried to restrain the Indians from attacking American settlers. Although the Americans would never believe it, this was in fact true. The British did not want an Indian war because they knew it would increase the chances of conflict between Britain and the United States. Nonetheless, they could not stop all supplies to the Indians, for this would completely end their influence over them.

The view of Fort George, Upper Canada (Niagara-on-the-Lake,
Ontario), from Old Fort Niagara, c. 1805.
[Courtesy of the Baldwin Room, Metropolitan Toronto Library.]

In 1811, the Americans drastically increased their pressure on
Indian lands. They were worried about Tecumseh's efforts to
unite the tribes. While Tecumseh was away in the south seeking
Indian support for the confederacy, Governor Harrison marched
an army into Indian territory near Prophetstown on the
Tippecanoe River. He planned to disperse the Indians from this
village because it was the centre of the Prophet's influence. At
dawn on November 7, the Prophet attacked the American troops.
After several hours of intense fighting, the Indians were defeated
and the Americans destroyed the town and its food supplies. The
destruction of Prophetstown provoked more Indian attacks instead of ending the warfare, but Indian resistance continued to
be weakened by disunity among the tribes.

Americans in the West continued to believe that British
contact with the Indians encouraged the fierce frontier warfare
in which settlers' families were killed and their farms destroyed.
This seemed to many to be reason enough to make war on Britain. Once the British were driven out of Canada, the Indians
would have no allies to help them defend their lands. Furthermore, American settlement of Upper Canada could continue
without hindrance or fear.

This view has been called the land expansionist cause of the war. It was expressed most strongly in the South and West, particularly in Ohio, Tennessee and Kentucky. In the election of 1810 for the United States Congress, many men with this view won seats from these states. Led by Henry Clay of Kentucky, they were aptly called "War Hawks" because they urged war against Britain.

The War Hawks gave other reasons for wanting war, and these reflected what was happening on the Atlantic coast. There the main issue between Britain and the United States was "maritime rights."

MARITIME RIGHTS

As we have seen, the Royal Navy was stopping neutral ships from entering ports under Napoleon's control. Most of these ships were from the United States, and for this reason many Americans concluded that the British were simply interfering with their very profitable trade. Even worse in their eyes was the Royal Navy's practice of stopping neutral ships at sea to search for contraband (goods which the British had declared illegal to trade with Europe) and deserters who had fled from the harsh and pitifully paid life on British warships. Many deserters took jobs on American ships, and the American government tried to protect them by giving them certificates of American citizenship. To British naval captains, however, these men had broken the law by deserting and could legally be returned to a British ship. Sometimes captains acted rashly and even impressed men who were native-born American citizens into service on British ships.

From the Americans' point of view, this arrogant British behaviour not only harmed their country's commerce, it defied American law and authority. Many believed that their nation's honour was being insulted and that war was the only way to make Britain respect American sovereignty.

Americans have sometimes called the War of 1812 their "second war of independence." Some felt strongly that the young nation had to go to war to prove it was truly independent. John Clopton of Virginia wrote:

> The outrages in impressing American seamen exceed
> all manner of description. Indeed the whole system of

aggression now is such that the real question between Great Britain and the United States has ceased to be a question merely relating to certain rights of commerce ... it is now clearly, positively, and directly *a question of independence,* that is to say, whether the United States are really an independent nation. [1]

Patriotism and nationalism added further reasons to go to war.

AMERICAN WEAKNESSES

Not all Americans agreed on the need for war, and those who did could not agree on how to fight it. Differences of opinion affected their preparations and the conduct of the campaigns and in the end, these disagreements were important in preventing the conquest of Canada.

The capture of Canada would require more and better troops than the Americans possessed in 1812. They had few regulars, that is, full-time, trained, professional soldiers and, more seriously, they lacked high ranking officers experienced in leading large bodies of men. The main American force was the militia made up of male citizens of fighting age who were required to serve in defence of their country for short periods. Usually, they had no training as soldiers and knew nothing of military organization and discipline.

As commander-in-chief of the armed forces, the president controlled the regulars but not the militia. He had to ask each state government to send its militia to fight. Many of these governments agreed with the militiamen in believing that they should not serve outside the state, and neither the president nor Congress had the authority to make them do so.

There were disagreements also between the main political parties (Federalist and Republican), between coastal and inland regions and between northern and southern states. Federalists, most of whom opposed war with Britain, were strong in New York and New England. The southern and western states were dominated by Republicans most of whom favoured war. This party of President Madison also controlled Congress. But the party wanted war on the cheap, for its members were against a large army and navy and also opposed increasing taxes to pay for a war. As a result, Congress voted for only a small expansion of the army

Peter B. Porter of New York was elected to Congress in 1809 and became a leader of the "War Hawks." As chairman of the House Committee on Foreign Affairs, he prepared a report advocating preparation for war with Great Britain. In December, 1812 he and General Smyth fought a duel on Grand Island in the Niagara River, during which neither man was harmed. He led New York and Pennyslvania militiamen and Indians at the battles of Chippawa and Lundy's Lane and during the siege of Fort Erie. After the war, he served as one of the commissioners who determined the boundary between Canada and the U.S.

[Courtesy of the Buffalo and Erie County Historical Society.]

— from 10,000 to 35,000 men. Planning to rely on less expensive volunteer forces, it gave the president the right to request 50,000 militia for one year's service and 100,000 for only six months. The politicians seemed unconcerned that these periods of service would not provide enough time to train recruits properly. Congress also voted down a larger navy and heavy tax increases. These votes meant the nation would not have a fleet to fight the Royal Navy and would have to borrow to pay for the war.

The uncertainty and confusion of the United States government reflected the deep divisions within the country. The British blockade and impressment of Americans affected mostly the people along the central and northern Atlantic coast. They owned the ships that were being stopped, and it was mainly their men who were being impressed. Yet these same people, particularly in New England, were the ones most fearful of war because they would be exposed to the power of the British navy. Moreover, many of these people made their living from trading and fishing, both of which the British navy could stop.

The inland and southern regions felt there was little danger to them from British forces. Perhaps their leaders were influenced by a report given early in 1812 to the United States Secretary of War which suggested that conquest would be easy because the British troops in Canada were "'much debilitated by intemperance'" and the Lower Canadian militia, "'the meanest among the refuse of men'" was unarmed and "trained only 'in drunken frolics on common week days.'"[2] People in those regions believed a successful war would enable them to export freely the products they grew, particularly cotton and tobacco, without interference from British warships. They also looked forward to the final defeat of the Indians.

When Congress voted on the declaration of war, it was divided: seventy-nine in favour to forty-nine against in the House of Representatives, nineteen to thirteen in the Senate. Opponents came mainly from New England, New York, and New Jersey, with a few from the South and West. This strange mixture of enthusiasm and reluctance for war foretold the tremendous difficulties that President Madison would face. New England not only voted against war but when the struggle came, even helped Britain. State governors would not allow their militia to go beyond their borders, thereby reducing the forces that could be fielded most easily against British North America. New Englanders would not lend money to their federal government — they would and did lend it to the British government. Farmers in New York and Vermont sold supplies to the British army in Canada, greatly helping Canada's defence. New England's opposition to the war also meant that there could be no land attack on New Brunswick and Nova Scotia. Since the United States did not have a large navy, it could not threaten those colonies from the sea.

CANADA'S WEAKNESSES

The Americans could attack the Canadas overland without much difficulty and, probably, with the advantage of surprise. There were differences of opinion among Canadians as to where the greatest danger threatened, but the government was worried only about Upper Canada. It had good reason because the majority of the colony's population had arrived from the United States after 1791. They may have numbered over 50,000 compared to about 13,000 descendants of Loyalists and about 15,000 immigrants from Britain. Would the former Americans defend British rule or would they welcome American troops? Sir George Prevost, governor of the Canadas, could not be certain, nor could Major General Isaac Brock, commander of the forces in Upper Canada. In May 1812, Prevost estimated the militia in Upper Canada at 11,000 but thought only 4,000 could be relied on to be loyal.

In Lower Canada the French Canadians would have no reason to welcome American invaders. There had been violent quarrels and bad feeling between French-Canadian political leaders and Governor James Craig, but that had changed when Prevost became governor in 1811. Prevost's ability to speak French, his charm and courtesy and his political experience, all qualified him to govern the troubled people of Lower Canada. He deliberately set about establishing good relations with French-Canadian leaders and the Roman Catholic church. As a result, the colony's assembly would strongly support his efforts to raise money and men for the defence of Lower Canada.

In 1811, Brock was appointed administrator as well as commanding officer of Upper Canada. This meant he had to look after civil government in place of the Lieutenant Governor, Sir Francis Gore, who preferred to be in England and remained there until the war was over. Brock, like Prevost, had to be concerned about civilian as well as military problems.

The principal military problem in 1812 was the small number of trained soldiers in Canada. There were only about 5,600 British regulars in all. Some 1,400 of these were in Upper Canada, where they had to guard the long frontier and garrison its seven forts as well as St. Joseph, 1,100 kilometres northwest of York. More forces were needed and an obvious source was the manpower of the colonies.

Already some men were serving as regulars in what were called "fencible" regiments. These were regiments raised among the settlers for local defence and trained to the British army's standard. An example was the Glengarry Light Infantry Fencibles which Prevost authorized in December 1811. The government began recruiting Scottish settlers, many of whom had been soldiers, from Glengarry County in Upper Canada, but the need for manpower led to recruiting in the maritime provinces. The other locally raised troops were the Canadian Fencibles, the Royal Newfoundland Regiment, the Provincial Corps of Light Infantry (raised among French-Canadians and popularly known as the Voltigeurs), the Nova Scotia Fencibles, and the New Brunswick Fencibles which became 104th Regiment of Foot on the regular establishment. Some of these units would fight in major battles and prove to be effective soldiers.

These regiments were all formed of volunteers as were the few cavalry corps, such as the Niagara Light Dragoons and the Canadian Light Dragoons. Cavalrymen had to be drawn from prosperous families because they had to provide their own horses. They were expected less to fight than to carry messages and scout the enemy.

Still more men were needed and, as in the United States, the Canadian government could draw on the militia. By law all males aged 16 to 60 belonged to it and were supposed to attend a few days of training every year. Attendance was generally poor and, in any case, that amount of training was far too little to be of value. This was only the beginning of the militia's problems, for they lacked virtually everything: weapons, ammunition, uniforms, tents, blankets, food, even boots and cooking pots.

At first, militia law made no provision for compensating the families of militiamen killed or wounded in action. Brock set out to change this situation by proposing that such families receive

The Provincial Corps of Light Infantry (Canadian Voltigeurs) was a
provincial corps, intended for local defence. It was raised in the
spring of 1812 by Major Charles-Michel d'Irrumberry de Salaberry, a
member of a prominent Quebec family and a regular soldier in the
British army. The Regiment saw a good deal of action from 1812 to
1814. Although best remembered for its victory at Chateauguay in
October 1813, men of this unit also fought in 1812 at Salmon River,
in 1813 at Sackets Harbor and Crysler's Farm and in 1814 at La Colle,
Odelltown and Plattsburg as well as in numerous border skirmishes.
The Voltigeurs were disbanded in March, 1815.
[Courtesy of Canadian Park Service.]

land as compensation; this was approved in 1812 by the British government. But while the men were away on militia duty, their families had to look after the farm or business which meant the burden fell upon the women, children, and old people. During the busiest times — seeding and harvesting — no one could be spared from the farm even if there was a war on. It was essential that the farm work be done in Upper Canada or people would go hungry.

Not surprisingly, militia in both Canada and the United States were always more concerned about their homes and farms than about military duties. These farmers and townsmen could not be expected to fight with the discipline or courage of regulars. Sometimes they did fight stubbornly, usually when defending their homes (as the Canadians were) rather than when attacking another country (as the Americans were). Fighting in war was the responsibility of the soldiers. Militiamen were meant to perform other duties such as transporting supplies, building roads and fortifications, and guarding prisoners. But the British commanders knew that if the Americans invaded, the Canadian militia would have to fight along with the army and Indians. They therefore set about improving the military ability of the militia.

In Lower Canada, a new Militia Act was passed in April 1812 providing for a Select Embodied Militia which was to be paid. In Upper Canada, the Militia Act was revised to create unpaid militia flank companies. These changes meant that part of each militia battalion would receive extra training to make them better soldiers. The Select Embodied Militia was made up of men chosen by lot from the Sedentary Militia, whereas the flank companies were composed of volunteers. In 1813 the Volunteer Incorporated Militia was created. Men volunteered to serve in it until the end of the war, received pay, and were promised land grants when the force was disbanded. All these special companies of militia would fight strongly in several major battles.

The need to use militia who remained civilians created extra problems for Prevost and Brock, for they could not simply give orders to civilians as they could to soldiers. They faced the need to persuade the elected assemblies in Lower and Upper Canada to change the militia laws, to vote money and to pass other laws to help the war effort.

Prevost had success with the Assembly of Lower Canada. Besides the new Militia Act, it voted to make a large sum of money

Lower Canada Embodied Militia had five battalions. First
embodied in May, 1812 by lot from Sedentary Militia, battalions
from this regiment fought at Chateauguay on October 26, 1813
and during the campaign against Plattsburgh in September, 1814.
It was disbanded in March, 1815.
[Courtesy of Parks Canada Service.]

available to him. After war broke out, he persuaded the assembly to vote more funds and to guarantee a paper currency called Army Bills. At that time, people believed that coins were the only safe money because the gold or silver of the coins had intrinsic value whereas paper money was risky even if backed by the government. However, under the influence of their political and religious leaders, Lower Canadians soon accepted the bills as safe. Prevost used them to buy supplies and pay militia wages as well as sending them to Upper Canada to help its government cover expenses.

Brock's prospects were decidedly bleak compared to Prevost's. In early 1812 Brock proposed several laws which would have strengthened his control over the province. The assembly was not willing in peace time to give him the powers he wanted, but it did amend the Militia Act and vote some money for the militia. In July, even though war had been declared, the assembly was again unwilling to agree to Brock's demands for a further strengthening of the militia law and the imposition of martial law (law established and enforced by military officers instead of by civilians). Brock's despair is evident in his letter of 28 July to Prevost:

> A more decent House has not been elected since the formation of the province — but I perceive at once that I shall get no good of them. They, like the magistrates and other in office, evidently mean to remain passive .... if I have recourse to the law martial I am told the whole armed force will disperse. Never was an officer placed in a more awkward predicament. [3]

In the North and West, and perhaps elsewhere, Indians might help in the defence of Canada. Even before the war, western Indians were gathering at Amherstburg. Robert Dickson, a British fur trader, was bringing others to St. Joseph. But the Six Nations, or Iroquois, on the Grand River did not want to get involved.

The Iroquois were not being threatened by the Americans as were the western Indians. In July, 1812, the Six Nation Indians living in the United States decided to take no part in the war. They urged the Six Nations on the Grand River to follow their example. This persuasion was not really needed, but it probably strengthened the desire of most of the Grand River Indians to be neutral. One of their leaders, John Norton (Teyoninhokarawen), wanted to support the British but not many Indians would follow him. Thus, Brock and Prevost could not count on having a large number of Canadian Iroquois warriors.

THE PROVINCIAL MARINE

There was another force which was important to the defence of the Canadas although we often forget about it. This was the Provincial Marine, consisting of warships on Lakes Champlain, Ontario and Erie. When war broke out, the British had naval control of these waters. On Lake Champlain they had a schooner, while the Americans had no warship. On Lake Ontario the British had six vessels, including the 22-gun *Royal George;* the Americans had only the 16-gun *Oneida,* though they soon bought six merchant schooners to convert to warships. On Lake Erie the British had the *Queen Charlotte* (16 guns), the *General Hunter* (6 guns) and during the summer launched the *Lady Prevost* (10 guns). The Americans had only one unarmed ship, the *Adams.*

Naval control of the lakes was important for several reasons. For one thing, ships were the fastest way to move supplies and troops. For another, British control of the lakes would force the Americans to attack along land routes into Upper Canada instead of anywhere they pleased. This simplified planning for Canada's defence. Moreover, if the Americans advanced far into Upper Canada, naval forces could cut their armies' lines of supply and communication. The British faced great problems of maintaining naval forces so far inland. Canada had few trained or experienced sailors and, in effect, depended for almost all of them on the overstretched Royal Navy. It would also have to supply the numerous items necessary to build and supply ships. But how could the British navy spare men and supplies when it had the more important roles of blockading Europe and, after June, 1812, the coast of the United States? By contrast, the United States had plenty of sailors and supplies to send to their naval bases of Plattsburg on Lake Champlain, Sackets Harbor on Lake Ontario, and Presque Isle on Lake Erie.

WAR IS DECLARED!

On June 1, Madison gave Congress five reasons for his war message. First was the impressment of American citizens into the British navy. Second, he complained of British ships off the coast stopping and searching American vessels. Third, was the British blockade by which, he said, "our commerce has been plundered in every sea". Fourth came the Orders in Council. The major reasons, it would appear, were maritime rights. Finally, Madison stated, "In reviewing the conduct of Great Britain towards the United States *our attention is necessarily drawn to the warfare just renewed by the savages on one of our extensive frontiers—*"[4] In other words, Madison blamed the British, not the Americans, for starting Indian warfare in the West!

On June 18 Congress passed a bill approving the President's call for war and Madison signed it. This officially began the War of 1812 although Britain did not declare war until January 9, 1813, almost seven months later. Meanwhile, as soon as the American decision was taken, messengers rode hastily north to Montreal and Newark.

A SUMMARY

While there were undoubted weaknesses in British North America's defences, there were also significant strengths at the outset of war. There was British naval control of the lakes, regulars commanded by good officers, and the western Indians, many led by the valiant Tecumseh. The militia was the weakest part of Canada's defenses, but steps were being taken to improve it.

Disagreements among Americans over the war were an enormous benefit to Canada. The defence was also helped by the poor leadership of the American army, which was not well trained at the beginning of the conflict, and by the reliance on often unpredictable state militias. President Madison did not provide firm direction for the political and military leaders who decided how the war was to be fought. As a result, the Americans time after time made the mistake of attacking west of Kingston instead of cutting the St. Lawrence route.

Upper Canada's principal weakness was dependence on that route with its disadvantages of rapids, winter freeze-up, and proximity to the American border.

2
A SURPRISING WAR, 1812

EUROPE

From Spain to Russia, Napoleon straddled Europe. By spring Europeans could see that he was preparing to attack Russia, for he was gathering troops from the countries he controlled directly as well as from his allies. Napoleon's Grand Army began the invasion in June and the Russians retreated. Even though the British knew that the Americans were making preparations for war, they were forced to give almost full attention to the spreading conflict on the continent.

The British commander, the Duke of Wellington, had been fighting the French in the Iberian Peninsula since 1809. In the spring of 1812, he began to win important victories, but it was clear that the French would not be driven out without a great deal more hard fighting. The British government would have to continue sending Wellington many soldiers and large amounts of supplies and money. There would be little to spare for war in North America.

Sensibly, the British government tried to avoid war with the Americans. Unfortunately, its move to repeal the Orders in

Council, the major source of disagreement, was delayed by the assassination in May of the Prime Minister Spencer Perceval. A new government could not be formed for some weeks because the major political leaders disagreed so strongly over policies. Eventually, Lord Liverpool formed a government and moved quickly to repeal the Orders on June 23.

NORTH AMERICA

But it was too late in North America. Still, the British avoided acting aggressively and delayed their declaration of war until January, 1813, in the hope that the Americans would rescind theirs. Thus, for more than six months, the British struggled with the problem of having to help British North America fight a war they wanted no part of while at the same time trying not to anger the United States so that fighting could soon be ended. President Madison, however, had no intention of changing his mind.

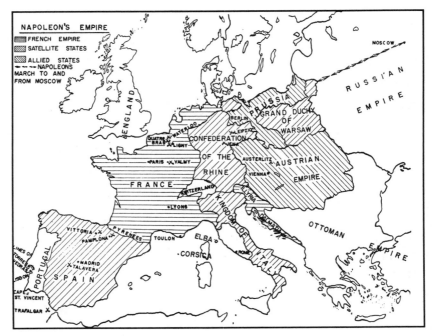

Napoleon's empire.

[Adapted from R.A. Preston, S.F. Wise, and H.O. Werner, Men in Arms: A History of Warfare and its Interrelationships with Western Society, *revised edition (New York, 1956), p. 185.]*

Governor Prevost, General Brock in Upper Canada, and Sir John Sherbrooke, commanding officer in the Maritimes, had realized early in 1811 that the threat of war was serious. They knew that Britain could spare them little aid and that they would have to defend the colonies with the forces and means they had available.

Sherbrooke had about 4,300 regulars, mostly in Nova Scotia. That colony had some 11,000 men in the militia, but only half of them were armed and trained. The New Brunswick militia was too scattered and untrained and the Prince Edward Island and Cape Breton militias were too small to count as military forces. Halifax, a major British naval base, was the only town in the Maritimes with fortifications which troops could use to defend it. Clearly, the primary defence of the Atlantic colonies in case of war would be the Royal Navy.

In the Canadas, Prevost and Brock considered their 5,600 troops too few. In addition to organizing training for militia units, they set about strengthening defences in several ways. Prevost asked Britain to send help, specifically requesting, for example, 10,000 muskets, 200 sabres, and saddles and bridles to equip cavalry. The two main regiments he had, the 49th and the 41st, were due to return to England. The government told Prevost that in the event of war, he could keep these regiments as well as those (the 103rd and the 1st, or Royal Scots) being sent as replacements.

During the spring and summer of 1812, Prevost sent what men and supplies he could spare to Upper Canada along with guns, money, and clothing. He asked Sherbrooke to send money and weapons from Halifax, and the first shipment of these arrived at Quebec in September. He also decided to keep the 100th Regiment, which was to have gone to Nova Scotia.

All this was good planning and is evidence of the professionalism of these British generals. On the American side, there was little of this kind of careful, detailed preparation. As a result, the President's authority to call out thousands of men would not be very effective in practice. Even when these forces were raised, they were not trained or properly supplied. Of course, the serious flaws of the American military structure were not evident to Canada's defenders and so they expected an early invasion by numerous and powerful forces.

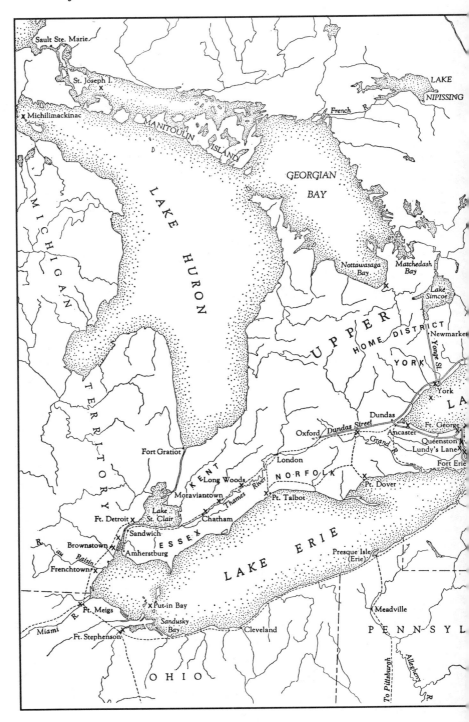

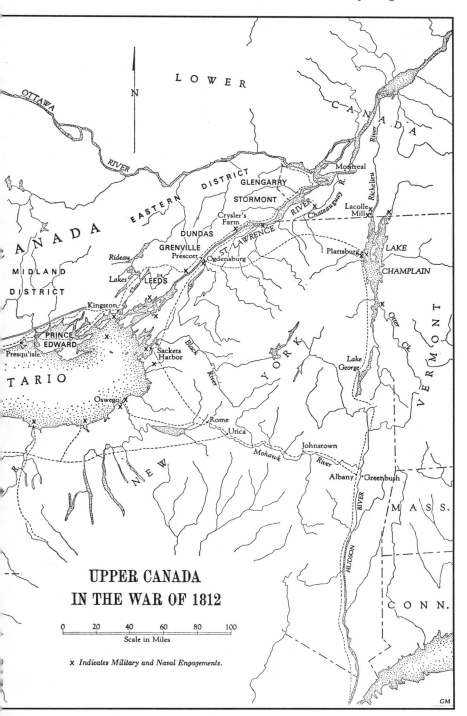

UPPER CANADA
IN THE WAR OF 1812

```
0    20    40    60    80   100
Scale in Miles
```

x *Indicates Military and Naval Engagements.*

eprinted from The Defended Border *by Morris Zaslow, (Toronto, Macmillan of Canada, 1964), pp. 4-5.]*

BRITISH STRATEGY

The Americans could easily invade Canada from northern New York state and cut the St. Lawrence Route or even attack Montreal. Or if their objective was limited to Upper Canada, they could threaten it from their bases at Michilimackinac, Detroit, and Fort Niagara. The point is that the Americans had the advantage of knowing when they intended to begin the war and, therefore, could choose where to gather forces and when to launch an invasion.

Clearly, it was vital to Prevost and Brock to know about American intentions and timing and they had informants gathering information. Canada's defenders had no desire to conquer American territory but simply to repel any invasion. If they were beaten back, it was accepted British strategic doctrine that their troops would retreat to Quebec City and at all costs, hold on to that fortress until succour could come from Great Britain.

But beyond that point, Brock and Prevost disagreed about strategy. Both before and after war was declared, Prevost opposed striking across the border at the enemy. He argued that a British attack would unite Americans in support of the war and would thereby increase the danger to Canada rather than eliminate it. Brock asserted that Upper Canada could be defended and insisted that vigorous efforts ought to be made to retain it. The most effective strategy, he argued, would be to attack the Americans in the West right at the outset of the war. Throw the Americans off balance rather than wait passively for them to strike first was his advice to Prevost.

Brock proposed to strengthen British forces at St. Joseph and Amherstburg and be ready to seize Michilimackinac and Detroit as soon as war broke out. He thought that victories early in the war were the only way to win the support of the Indians. He also hoped that early defeats might discourage the Americans, who expected an easy victory. A setback might make them less willing to face the continued expense and difficulties of warfare. Moreover, if the British won battles in the West, the Americans would be forced to concentrate their efforts there rather than against the vital St. Lawrence route. The defenders would thus gain time — time to organize and train militia, time for Britain to send aid across the ocean. It was the Americans who had to hurry before more British troops reached Canada and before the Royal Navy could attack the American coast.

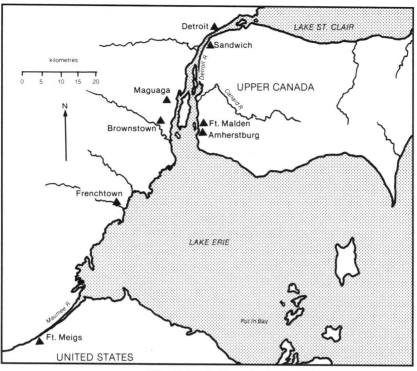

The Detroit frontier.
[Reprinted from The War of 1812: The War For Canada, *by W.B. Turner (Toronto, Grolier Limited, 1982), p. 26.]*

Compared to battles in Europe, those in North America were short and fought by tiny armies. Yet these first clashes were important because Britain could not quickly reinforce her colonies. Canada's fate really did hang on the battles of 1812.

Others, besides British army commanding officers, were anxious to know when war was declared. One group vitally interested in this news was the fur traders of Montreal whose valuable cargoes moved along the Great Lakes and St. Lawrence. War would interrupt their trade and the Americans might seize their trade goods and furs. To avoid this danger, the Montreal merchants could use other routes which would be safer even if longer and more expensive.

The merchants had business partners in New York City who sent word to Canada as soon as they heard of Madison's declaration of war. The message reached Montreal on June 24 and was taken next day to Prevost at Quebec. Brock received the news at

York on June 25 and immediately sent messages to the western forts. They reached Lieutenant Colonel Thomas St. George, the commander at Fort Malden, on June 28 and Captain Charles Roberts at St. Joseph on July 8. These British officers acted on the declaration of war before their American opponents even knew about it.

HULL'S INVASION OF CANADA

Meanwhile, Brigadier General William Hull was leading a force of over 2,000 American regulars and militia towards Detroit. The men struggled through pathless, thick forests in pouring rain. At last, on June 29, they emerged from the dark woods onto the shore of Lake Erie 130 kilometres from Detroit. By this time, many were too sick to continue the march and so Hull hired a ship, the *Cayahoga,* to transport them the rest of the way. He also put his papers containing his instructions and the list of his men on the ship. He did not know that war had been declared and that the British were waiting.

On July 3, the *General Hunter* captured the *Cayahoga.* Hull's papers were immediately sent to Brock who thus learned Hull's orders and the size of his army. The British general skilfully used that knowledge to his advantage.

Two days after the capture, Hull reached Detroit which was a village of 800 people surrounded by stout wooden walls four metres high. Behind it stood a fort with strong walls, cannon and a garrison of about 100. Every day more and more Michigan militiamen arrived. There could be no doubt that Hull's force and position were much stronger than those of the British who had about 300 regulars, 800 militia from Kent and Essex counties and perhaps 300 Indians.

The war truly began on July 12 when Hull crossed the river and occupied Sandwich, thus launching the first invasion of Canada. The men camped on Colonel Jean Baptiste Baby's farm and Hull moved into the Colonel's "beautiful mansion."[1]

Hull planned to capture Fort Malden before advancing further east. He did not move against the fort immediately, however, for two reasons. He expected he would have to use cannon and was waiting until wheeled carriages were made. Also he was hoping that the Canadian militia would return home or come

Private, 10th Royal Veteran Battalion, 1812. A regular unit composed of older soldiers. Most were stationed at Halifax, Nova Scotia, but some men participated in actions at Michilimackinac and Frenchtown.
[Courtesy of Canadian Park Service.]

over to his side. To discourage them from fighting he sent out a proclamation:

> Inhabitants of Canadas!... The army under my command has invaded your country .... To the peaceable, unoffending inhabitants, it brings neither danger nor difficulty .... I come to protect, not to injure you...In the name of my country, and by the authority of my government, I promise protection to your persons, property, and rights. Remain at your homes .... raise not your hands against your brethren .... The United States offer you peace, liberty and security. Your choice lies between these and war, slavery and destruction.[2]

He added that his force was strong enough to conquer the province and warned that anyone fighting alongside the Indians against his army would be killed. He also sent agents to tell the Grand River Indians they would be left alone if they remained neutral.

Many Canadian militiamen did go home, and at least 60 deserted to the American army. By July 15, St. George found that half his militia had left and he did not think the remainder would be reliable. Chief Norton could promise only 40 to 50 warriors from the Grand River, for most of the Six Nations remained neutral.

Hull and his army were nonetheless in more danger than they realized. Upper Canada's defences were in strong hands.

THE CAPTURE OF MICHILIMACKINAC AND ITS CONSEQUENCES

Far to the north, at St. Joseph, Captain Roberts had only 45 soldiers, whereas Lieutenant Porter Hanks at Michilimakinac had 61 regulars in a sturdier fort. But Roberts knew that Brock expected him to act vigorously and what defence was more effective than an unexpected attack?

The North West Company fur traders were very willing to help him. The company provided a ship and 180 Canadian voyageurs whom Roberts took along with his soldiers and about 400 Indians. His men landed on Michilimackinac Island at 3 a.m. on July 17. Dragging a small cannon, they climbed a hill overlooking the fort and about two hours before noon, Roberts called upon the Americans to surrender. Hanks gave up without a fight. His position was hopeless, and he feared that if he lost the battle, the Indians might kill everyone in the fort. This American fear of Indians killing prisoners would again and again affect the course of battles. It increased the effectiveness of the Indians as British allies and decreased American desire to fight.

This small victory had great consequences. Hull received the distressing news at Sandwich on August 2. That same day, Wyandot Indians who lived near Detroit crossed the river to join the British. Robert's success was bearing fruit quickly by gaining the British many allies among Indians in the Michigan Territory.

William Hull was a civilian who had last seen military service in the American Revolution thirty years earlier. He had not held high rank then and had been appointed to lead the North Western Army because of his status as governor of the Michigan Territory, not because of military ability. He did not want the appointment and never showed the drive of his British opponents.

Before Michilimackinac, Hull had sent raiding parties into Upper Canada and his men had clashed with the British along the Canard River south of Sandwich. Now the whole position had changed. Hull wrote to the governors of Ohio and Kentucky asking for reinforcements, and to the Secretary of War in Washington expressing his fears that masses of Indians would attack Detroit. He dispatched the letters under a guard of a 200-man force that he was sending to escort a supply column from Ohio. At Brownstown, Indians led by Tecumseh ambushed the Americans, who fled back to Detroit. This attack increased Hull's fears. Even more important, his letters were captured and sent to Brock.

Brock had been busy ever since he had learned of the declaration of war. He instructed the militia along the St. Lawrence to be ready to meet an attack. He called out the flank companies of the Lincoln militia to reinforce the 41st Regiment along the Niagara River. He did not fear an American attack there at this time, but he wanted to show both Americans and Canadians that the province would be defended.

About 800 militiamen turned out and Brock put most of them on guard duty along the Niagara. But they soon became concerned about getting in the harvest, and by mid-July, Brock was forced to allow half of them to return to their farms.

As the bad news of Hull's invasion and of militia desertions came from the West, Brock began to fear that nothing could stop Hull from marching eastward. What could be done, he did. He sent Colonel Henry Procter to take command at Amherstburg and issued a proclamation of his own, defending British rule in Canada and warning that American control would bring oppression. For the moment, he could not take more positive action such as going to Amherstburg himself because he was required to meet the legislature in York.

Brock felt terribly frustrated by being tied down with politics at York, but instead of giving way to despair, he acted decisively and positively. His attitude was best summed up by his own comment: "Most of the people have lost all confidence—I however speak loud and look big."[3]

At last, came the encouraging news: Roberts had captured Michilimackinac. As soon as Brock ended the meeting of the legislature, he hurried to the Grand River. On August 7, he talked to a council of the Indians who promised to send warriors to help him. By evening, he reached Port Dover, on Lake Erie, where militia and regulars were gathering. The next day, most of the force embarked in small boats for Amherstburg.

They had over 300 kilometres to travel on a lake where storms could blow up quickly. Fierce rain and wind almost stopped their progress but Brock pushed on day and night until they reached Amherstburg late on the thirteenth. When General Hull heard that Brock was on his way, he took most of his army back across the river to Detroit. On August 9, he sent another force, larger this time, to escort the supply train. They were ambushed near the village of Maguaga by regulars, militia, and Indians under Tecumseh. The Americans drove off the attackers, but instead of pushing on to meet the supply column, they camped where they were. After a night spent in pouring rain without tents, they returned to Detroit. More than ever, Hull feared enemies were all around him. He recalled the rest of his troops from Upper Canada, thus ending the first American invasion.

BROCK AND TECUMSEH WIN A GREAT VICTORY

Soon after arriving at Amherstburg, Brock met Tecumseh. Each impressed the other and a real friendship seems to have been

46

born. There is a legend that Tecumseh turned to his followers and said of Brock, "This is a man."[4] Brock later wrote, "He who attracted most my attention was a Shawnee chief, Tecumseh...a more sagacious or a more gallant warrior does not I believe exist. He was the admiration of everyone who conversed with him."[5] (Ironically, the two most courageous leaders in this war would both be killed in defence of their cause.)

The next day, Brock held a conference with his officers, Tecumseh and other Indian chiefs, at which he outlined his plan to attack Detroit. Colonel Procter opposed it, thinking the risk too great. Having read the captured letters, however, Brock knew the state of Hull's mind. He concluded that the Americans had lost confidence in their general and would not be eager to fight. Tecumseh supported Brock's plan.

Brock sent a demand to Hull for immediate surrender. Knowing the American fear of Indians, he warned that the warriors might get out of control in a fight. Hull rejected the demand.

British cannon at Sandwich began firing at Detroit and the Americans shot back, but neither side did much damage. During the night of August 15, about 600 Indians crossed the river. Early the next morning, Brock took 330 regulars and 400 militia across. The guns of the *Queen Charlotte* and the *General Hunter* covered the landing, but Hull had left the river bank unguarded.

Brock marched his little army towards the fort. Some of his militia were dressed in soldiers' tunics which made Hull think he faced mostly regulars. As the British advanced, they could see American gunners standing by their cannon awaiting the order to fire. Brock's force was in the open and cannon fire would have shredded their ranks. Brock seemed to have put his force in a very dangerous position.

Hull thought himself in even greater danger. During the morning, British shells had landed in the fort killing several men. The Americans had seen what appeared to be 2,000-3,000 Indians crossing an opening in the woods. In fact, Tecumseh had cleverly marched the same group of warriors through the clearing three times. The American commander was not at the wall giving orders or vigorously organizing the defence. Physically sick and mentally disordered, he simply sat on an old tent in a corner of the fort chewing tobacco.[6]

Suddenly, Brock and his men saw a white flag go up. They were amazed. Without consulting his officers, Hull had decided to surrender. The American general gave up everything in his command: the fort, its garrison, and even the troops outside. An American army of almost 2,200 men (nearly 600 of them regulars), along with 35 cannon, 2,500 muskets, 500 rifles, ammunition and the brig *Adams* were taken. Brock proclaimed British rule over the entire Michigan Territory. Soon afterwards, British regulars and militia marched south and took possession of American supplies and destroyed blockhouses as far south as the Maumee (Miami) River.

Brock issued a general order praising the regulars and militia while also recognizing the important role of Tecumseh and the Indians. Together, these two men had accomplished a great victory, but they would never see each other again.

American strategy in the West lay in ruins. The Americans had lost all posts north of the Maumee, their main army in the region and any hope of influencing the Indians. The weapons and supplies taken would be of great help in the defence of Upper Canada.

On the Canadian side morale soared, for people began to believe that the province could be defended and that American conquest was not going to be so easy after all. Michael Smith, a recent American immigrant who had travelled extensively in Upper Canada while compiling information for a book about the colony, wrote at the time,

> After this event, the people of Upper Canada became fearful of disobeying the government ... and the friends of the United States were discouraged and those of the King encouraged. The army now became respectable, and a dread fell on those who had opposed the government. The people now saw that it was as much as their property and lives were worth to disobey orders, and now what they had been compelled to do, after a while they did from choice.[7]

The government no longer had to tolerate a pro-American attitude among the people and could begin to insist that every man perform militia duty when called upon. Also affected were the Grand River Indians. Norton and his warriors had not played a large role at Detroit. Now the Six Nations began to drop their policy of neutrality and actively support the government, with very important consequences.

General Hull was to face a court martial a year and a half later. The court dropped the charge of treason but found him guilty of cowardice and neglect of duty. He escaped the sentence of execution by firing squad because President Madison pardoned him on the grounds of his Revolutionary War service.

BROCK ON THE NIAGARA FRONTIER

Brock hurried back to the Niagara frontier, perhaps fearful of what he might find. The news was good. Prevost had sent another general officer, Major General Roger H. Sheaffe, to assist him along with more regulars, including the 49th. With the province's defences thus strengthened, Brock wanted more than ever to strike at the Americans. In particular, he wanted to attack Sackets Harbor in order to prevent the creation there of an effective American naval force on Lake Ontario. His plans were blocked by a cease-fire and by Prevost's orders.

Prevost had proposed a cease-fire when he heard that Britain had repealed the Orders in Council and wanted to stop the fighting. Major General Henry Dearborn, the American commander for the area from Montreal to the Niagara River, readily agreed because he was far from ready to launch an invasion.

Henry Dearborn was another example of a politician appointed to military command because of his political prominence rather than his military talents. As a military leader, he acted slowly and was easily discouraged. Perhaps he was not as bad as Hull, but he achieved so little that Madison would finally dismiss him in July 1813.

The truce, which did not cover Hull's army, took effect on August 9. President Madison, however, refused to agree to it with the result that it terminated on September 4. Still, Dearborn was not ready to attack Canada.

When the cease-fire ended, Brock expected the Americans, who were growing in number every day, would quickly attack on the Niagara frontier. But he did not realize the extent of the problems in the enemy's camp such as widespread sickness among the men and a severe shortage of food and weapons. The militia, untrained and discontented, wanted only to return to their farms while regular officers would not cooperate with militia commanders. Disunity at higher levels worked to Canada's advantage. Peter B. Porter, a prominent New York politician and militia commander, complained bitterly to Secretary of War Eustis, "For God's sake, arouse and put forth the energies of the nation. The poor but patriotic citizens of ... the frontiers of New York are ... alone called out because their march to the frontier is shorter .... while the rich inhabitants of Pennsylvania are lolling in security and ease."[8]

Even though Brock was made aware of the American difficulties from deserters, he did not relax. He called up more militia to patrol the river. He organized a system of beacons to send messages across the peninsula from lake to lake. The weapons captured at Detroit were distributed and the cannon mounted along the river. Niagara Dragoons were told to be ready at a moment's notice to carry messages. Each detachment of troops had orders to march to the aid of the others if they received a call for help. In short, these small forces were being organized in a professional way to provide effective defence.

THE BATTLE OF QUEENSTON HEIGHTS

By early October, Brock had fewer than 1,000 regulars, about 600 militia, and a reserve of perhaps 600 militia and Indians. American forces opposite numbered about 6,000, over half of them regulars. They had also been joined by over 100 Seneca Indians from New York State who had decided to abandon neutrality. Another 2,000 Pennsylvania militia were on their way. The commander of the Niagara frontier, General Stephen Van Rensselaer, now had no good reasons for delaying an attack.

Van Rensselaer's plan was to cross the Niagara River from Lewiston and capture the village of Queenston which lay at the base of the Niagara Escarpment. Here, although the current was swift and the banks high, the river was narrow, Van Rensselaer wanted to gain control of the heights because this would cut the middle of Brock's defensive line. Queenston seemed vulnerable because, he knew, there were few troops there as Brock had concentrated forces at Fort George, Chippawa and Fort Erie. Brigadier General Alexander Smyth, who commanded 1,650 regulars at Buffalo, thought the plan foolish. He wanted to cross above the Falls, where the river was wider but calmer and its banks lower. Not getting his way, Smyth simply refused to cooperate with Van Rensselaer.

The omens for success were not good and they worsened on the night of October 10. The boats for the crossing were assembled opposite Queenston but the oars for them had to be brought upriver and that boat somehow ended upon the Canadian shore, whereupon the American officer in charge promptly disappeared! Brock knew of this abortive attempt but still thought the real attack would be against the extreme ends of his line, Fort George or Fort Erie.

The American invasion finally began about 4 a.m. on October 13. Three hundred militia under Colonel Solomon Van Rensselaer (the general's cousin) and 300 regulars under Lieutenant Colonel John Chrystie quietly climbed into boats to be rowed across the river.

This battle, like so many others, was not fought as the commanders on each side expected or planned. Three of the boats were caught by the current and carried downstream to the Canadian shore, their men becoming the first prisoners of the day. Other boats turned back. Not all the original force got across the river, but enough did to establish a small beachead.

As the Americans landed and tried to climb up the steep river bank, they were shot at by the troops of the 49th and 2nd York Militia flank company. They could not advance up the steep and slippery slope in the face of this fire but neither could the defenders drive them away from the shelter of the bank. Casualties mounted, and they included Colonel Van Rensselaer who returned wounded to the United States, leaving Captain John E. Wool in command.

Boats continued to cross bringing reinforcements and taking back wounded as the sky grew brighter and the mist began to disappear. Meanwhile, American cannon above Lewiston battered Queenston with their shot. A British cannon placed halfway up the escarpment in a redan fired back, while another at Vrooman's Point (over a kilometre north of Queenston) shelled the boats. Even if a boat was not hit directly, it could be damaged and men killed by a cannonball skipping across the water.

At Fort George, Brock heard the noise of battle. He mounted his horse Alfred (given him by Governor Craig) and rode for

Queenston telling militia units along the way to follow him. On arrival, he immediately rode up to the redan. Just as he dismounted, American troops appeared above him. Captain Wool had discovered a path leading up the rugged cliff to the top and left unguarded. A hail of musket fire drove Brock and the artillerymen down the hill, leaving the redan in American hands.

Brock did not know how long the Americans had been on the heights nor their strength there. He did know that unless he could drive them away and recapture that commanding position, the day could end in American victory.

In the village, Brock rallied his forces and, sword in hand, led them uphill. Slipping on the wet leaves, the British advanced while the Americans fired from behind trees and logs. Suddenly, one of the enemy stood up, aimed carefully and fired. The ball hit Brock in the chest and he fell dying to the ground.

Brock's aide-de-camp, Lieutenant Colonel John Macdonell, led another charge. It too was thrown back and Macdonell was severely wounded. (He died the next day.) The British retreated taking Macdonell with them but left Brock's body in a house in Queenston. They halted a kilometre or two north of the village to await help from Fort George. The Americans now controlled the heights above the village, and no force stood in the way of their advance down the escarpment. But they went no further that day. Despite their dramatic success, they did not gain a victory.

The Americans failed partly because of poor leadership: their troops were not sure exactly what they were supposed to do and were not given clear orders as the battle unfolded. There was no well organized system of sending over reinforcements. Many New York militiamen began to claim they could not be forced to leave the state. As well, the cannon at Vrooman's was still firing and only a few boats were getting across.

Probably the main factor preventing a further American advance was the presence of Indians on the heights. They skirmished with the Americans among the trees in the area where Brock's monument now stands on Queenston Heights. The Americans killed and wounded a few natives but did not drive them away, nor try very hard to do so. Some of the militia were so terrified they even tried to recross to their own side. Over there, panic ran through the militia ranks. The sight of wounded men being brought back and the sound of Indian war cries ended any

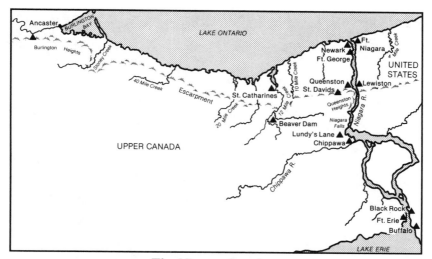

The Niagara frontier.
[Reprinted from The War of 1812: The War For Canada, *by W.B. Turner (Toronto, Grolier Limited, 1982), p.49.]*

desire they had to invade Canada. The American force on the heights, between 1,000 and 1,600 strong, was left on its own.

American delay gave General Sheaffe time to bring up troops and cannon from Fort George. He took most of his men inland around Queenston and up the escarpment. There he waited for forces from Chippawa. Between 3 and 4 p.m., he was ready with about 900 regulars plus Indians and militia (York, Lincoln, and Captain Runchey's Company of Coloured Men). They charged, and within minutes the battle was over. Some Americans were killed, others leaped over the cliff trying to escape. Over 900 surrendered and some 500 were casualties. British and Indian losses were reported as 19 killed and 77 wounded.

The battle of Queenston Heights was the last big American attempt to invade Canada in 1812. The British victory gave a tremendous boost to the morale of the defenders. Yet the price was high, for Brock had been killed.

No other British commander inspired as much affection and respect. In the short time between June and October 1812, Brock had proven that the Americans could be beaten, that numbers alone meant nothing. He had set an example of determination to both British and Canadians. Sheaffe actually won the battle, but this achievement was overshadowed by Brock's foolishly heroic charge that led to his death.

Brock dying at the Battle of Queenston Heights.
[Courtesy of the Archives of Ontario, S17866b.]

One reason people came to idealize Brock was the contrast between his leadership and that of his successor. Sheaffe took over as commander of the forces and administrator of Upper Canada. He immediately proposed a three-day truce to allow each side to bury their dead, look after the wounded and exchange prisoners. There was nothing unusual in making such a truce, but Sheaffe made the mistake of agreeing to continue it when the Americans asked. Many Canadians along the frontier thought this showed weakness and benefitted the Americans, who needed time to reorganize. They believed Sheaffe was willing to abandon Fort Erie and even retreat from the Niagara River. By December, several local leaders had lost confidence in him and put their thoughts in a letter to Prevost. Sheaffe never would be the dynamic, inspiring leader Brock had been.

GENERAL SMYTH'S WAR

The Americans felt frustrated and discouraged because twice their armies had been beaten and captured by smaller British-Canadian forces. Yet they still had more troops than the de-

"Reveille" for the Canadian Voltigeurs.
[Courtesy of Canadian Park Service.]

fenders and could easily increase their strength. Van Rensselaer resigned the command to Brigadier General Smyth who proved even less capable.

Smyth ended the truce on November 20 as his forces increased to about 5,000 men. At the end of the month, he made two separate attempts to invade Canada and bungled both. In the second effort, some 1,500 soldiers climbed into boats but Smyth recalled them before they could even cross the river. The men were wet, cold, tired and hungry. No wonder some began shooting at the general's tent! Smyth, complaining that his health was bad, went home. The government did not allow him to return to the army.

LATE 1812 CAMPAIGNS IN THE CANADAS

In November, General Dearborn finally moved against Canada. He marched 6,000 regulars and militia north from Plattsburg and they began crossing the border on the 20th. The defenders had plenty of warning. Lieutenant Colonel Charles de Salaberry led his Canadian Voltigeurs and 300 Mohawks to meet the enemy. Not far to the rear Major General Francis de Rottenburg commanded more than 5,000 regulars and militia, but they were not needed that day. The Voltigeurs and Indians clashed with the Americans, who became confused and began firing at each other. The Vermont and New York Militia refused to cross the border. Dearborn recalled his troops and retreated to Plattsburg, ending his campaigning for the year.

The only promising development for the Americans occurred on Lake Ontario. Captain Isaac Chauncey of the United States Navy arrived at Sackets Harbor in October to take command of American naval efforts on Lakes Ontario and Erie. Men and supplies were waiting for him and he set to work to create a strong naval force. By November 8, he was ready with seven warships. He chased the *Royal George* into Kingston harbour but could not attack it because of the guns on shore. The *Royal George*, however, had to remain there, and other vessels at York, until winter ended the navigation season. In effect, Chauncey controlled Lake Ontario at the end of 1812. His force was increased by the launching of the 24-gun *Madison* on November 26. It was bigger and carried more guns than any other ship on the lake.

THE WAR AT SEA

What had happened in the Maritime colonies during 1812? Very little. Sherbrooke learned on June 29 of the declaration of war and, at the same time, that his neighbours in New England wanted to continue normal trade. He issued a proclamation forbidding warfare against New England either on land or sea. But these good neighbourly attitudes did not last.

In June, the United States government authorized the licensing of privateers and, after President Madison refused to agree to a truce, the British government ordered the same action. This meant that private ship owners could get a licence to arm their vessels and raid enemy shipping. Privateers rarely attacked warships. They preferred the less risky and more profitable merchant ships of the enemy. Captured ships and their cargoes would be sold and the captors would receive a share of the money.

Both sides made use of privateers because governments would not have to spend money on warships and crews but, instead, could rely on the profit motive to spur ship owners and sailors. The Americans sent out some 500 privateers, two hundred of whom brought in over 1,300 prizes while, simultaneously, U.S. Navy ships brought in 165. From New Brunswick and Nova Scotia, more than 30 privateers sailed and returned with over 200 captures. All this warfare interfered with ocean commerce and made some people wealthy but did little to defeat either opponent.[9]

Royal Navy warships had begun patrolling the American coast as soon as war was declared. They did not intend to stop all shipping but rather to catch American privateers or warships that sailed out. A few vessels of the small American navy managed to slip past the British patrols and soon began to capture merchant vessels and even British warships. In July, a British squadron failed to catch the U.S. Navy frigate *Constitution* after chasing it for three days. The next month, the *Constitution* fought the British frigate *Guerriere* in the first major sea battle of the war. For over two hours they fired at each other until the *Guerriere* surrendered. This single-ship victory was followed by others during 1812 and made Americans proud of their navy. It showed that individual ships of the most powerful navy in the world could be beaten. Such victories would not defeat the Royal Navy or win the war, but the successes of the *Constitution*, the *United States*, the *Essex*, and the *Wasp* contrasted with the miserable failures of American armies.

THE PEOPLE AND THE WAR

How had the war affected the people of British North America? Those in the Maritime colonies noticed little difference except an increase in naval and military activity at Halifax—which meant more business for merchants.

In Lower Canada, more people were affected because Prevost called out the militia. In a few parishes near Montreal some men at first refused to serve, but in general the militia muster proceeded peacefully. Lower Canada suffered no destruction in 1812. Rather, there was increased prosperity for farmers, merchants and tavern keepers doing business with the British forces.

It was in Upper Canada that the Americans inflicted property damage and casualties. Neither was great, but the attacks and losses affected the attitudes of the people and government towards the war. At first many people hoped to be neutral or even favoured the Americans. They began to change this view as they experienced invasion and as their militiamen were killed, wounded, and/or captured.

Once the fighting began, the Upper Canadian government was able to take stronger action against those who refused to serve in the militia or who declared support for the United States. After the victory at Detroit, Brock proclaimed that any militiaman refusing to take the oath of allegiance would be punished. In November, Sheaffe set up boards to question people who claimed to be United States citizens and, therefore, exempt from military duty. The boards were to decide whether these people would be sent across the border or allowed to remain in Upper Canada.

Loyal residents of Upper Canada began to express their feelings more openly. In December, the Loyal and Patriotic Society was formed at York to provide winter clothing for the militia. Later in the war, it would give help to people who had suffered from the fighting. It would be supported by donations from Upper Canadians and from people in other colonies and in Britain.

By the end of 1812 two ideas were developing among Upper Canadians which contributed to a sense of patriotism. One was the regard for Brock as a great "Canadian" hero. The other is known as the "militia myth". It was the belief that the Canadian militia, rather than British regulars or Indians, were mainly responsible for saving Upper Canada from American conquest. This notion may have arisen as a result of a speech which Reverend John Strachan gave at York:

> It will be told by the future Historian, that the Province of Upper Canada, without the assistance of men or arms, except a handful of regular troops, repelled its invaders, slew or took them all prisoners, and captured from its enemies the greater part of the arms by which it was defended .... Our militia ... have twice saved the country.[10]

In reality, the militia's role in 1812 had been small. Throughout the war, in fact, the militia would be a significant factor in winning battles on only a few occasions. But it was these occasions that Canadians remembered and later exaggerated. Whatever the exact truth, two legends were born in 1812 and would grow to become part of Canadian nationalism.

No one could have predicted that by the end of 1812 Upper and Lower Canada would survive unconquered; indeed, not only unconquered but also with the inhabitants inspired to greater defensive efforts because several American invasions had been decidedly repulsed. What had looked like overwhelming United States superiority in military manpower supported by many industrial, logistical and strategic advantages, had been astonishingly ill-used or mis-directed during 1812. But, in 1813, would this fumbling continue or would the republic gain the victory that seemed so easily within its reach?

─3─
WAR ON LAND AND SEA, 1813

I N EUROPE, THE YEAR 1812 had ended disastrously for Napoleon. He had invaded Russia but had failed to destroy the Russian army or force the government to surrender. He had captured Moscow, but had found it abandoned and burning. In October, with winter approaching and no way to supply his troops, Napoleon had ordered them back to France. He had taken over 400,000 men into Russia; fewer than 100,000 had survived the appalling conditions of the long march home.

Leaving the tattered remnants of his retreating Grand Army in December, Napoleon had hurried back to Paris to raise more troops. He remained a strong threat to France's neighbours and no one could be sure if 1813 would see him again achieve domination of Europe or go down to defeat.

Except for a brief truce in the summer, the war would drag on through 1813. The greatest battle of the Napoleonic wars would be fought for three days in October around Leipzig in Germany. Napoleon would be defeated and would retreat to France but still refuse to surrender. This would mean that the war would have to be taken into France itself. In Spain, Wellington's troops (receiving a good deal of their food from New England) would doggedly drive the French northwards to the Franco-Spanish border. Before the end of the year, he would invade France from the south and allied armies would attack across the Rhine River.

THE BRITISH BLOCKADE THE AMERICAN COAST

In spite of the continuing demands on Britain for the war in Europe, that country was able to spare more attention and resources to the war in America. During 1813, British naval forces would become more active and aggressive. In January, Admiral John Warren was ordered to raid the American coast, especially around Chesapeake Bay. This area included many rich farms, important towns, including the capital of Washington, and naval bases. It was also an area where desire for war had been very strong. Warren soon imposed a strict blockade all the way from New York to the Gulf of Mexico. His vessels could not stop all United States Navy warships from sailing out, but they won fewer single-ship victories in 1813.

Still, Americans could be proud of the exploits of the *Hornet* in the Pacific and of the *Argus* off the coast of Britain itself. One of the most famous single-ship actions took place in June between the American *Chesapeake* and the Royal Navy's *Shannon*. The *Shannon*, under Captain Philip Broke, waited for the *Chesapeake* to come out of Boston harbour. When she did, the *Shannon* opened fire and after only 15 minutes the American vessel surrendered. The casualties included Captain James Lawrence of the *Chesapeake*, who ordered as he died, "'Don't give up the ship!'"[1] and Captain Broke who was seriously wounded. No less than three heroes are remembered from this battle: Lawrence for the Americans, Broke for the British and Wallis for the Nova Scotians. Provo William Parry Wallis, born in Halifax 22 years earlier, was second lieutenant of the *Shannon*. With the Captain wounded and the first lieutenant dead, it fell upon Wallis to take command of the ship and bring her, with the captured *Chesapeake*, into Halifax harbour where the people lined the shore to cheer both the victory and the man.[2] Wallis went on to a glorious career in the Navy and ended by becoming an Admiral before he died at age 101! The success of the *Shannon* showed that Americans could no longer count on winning single-ship battles.

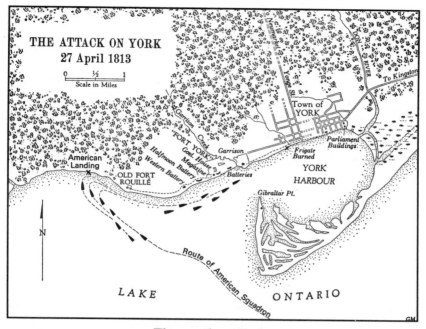

The attack on York.
[*Reprinted from* The Defended Border *by Morris Zaslow,*
(Toronto, Macmillan of Canada, 1964), p. 255.]

Much more important was the effect of the blockade, for it strangled American trade. This reduced the amount of taxes collected and therefore the amount of money available to the American government for fighting the war. Naval power thus played an important part in the war in more ways than one.

THE WAR ON THE INLAND LAKES

Naval development on the lakes would greatly affect the land war during 1813. American success on Lake Erie would lead to victories by their army on land. But on the more important Lake Ontario, the British would not lose, and this was crucial to their ability to hold on to most of Upper Canada.

The Provincial Marine, which was controlled by the army, had too few trained or experienced seamen. Prevost asked the government to send more and even wanted the Royal Navy to take control on the lakes. In May, this was done when the British Navy sent 450 seamen, 36 officers and a new commander for the lakes, Sir James Lucas Yeo. He had entered the Navy at age 11 and during his 20 years' service, had taken part in several naval battles. He would prove a most skilful, though cautious, commander of naval forces.

At Kingston and York, during the winter of 1812-1813, construction of warships hurried ahead. These were to have 24 guns each so that they could match the *Madison*. Chauncey started an even larger vessel at Sackets Harbor. A pattern developed of each side trying to out-build the other on the lakes. The Americans had the advantage of plenty of supplies, good shipbuilders, and seamen. Naval personnel and equipment for Canada had to come from Halifax and even England. Both sides knew that such aid would be limited while the war with Napoleon dragged on.

The naval contest on Lake Ontario would differ from that on Lakes Erie and Champlain. On those lakes, decisive naval battles were to be fought which in both cases would result in American victories. On Ontario, Yeo's and Chauncey's fleets would sail near each other but they would avoid a major engagement, preferring instead to attack each other's naval bases and supply depots.

The first raid was made by the Americans against York on April 27. In addition to the prestige of capturing the provincial capital, the Americans hoped to take the vessels in the harbour and destroy the ship under construction there. Despite the importance of York, its garrison was small (about 300 regulars, 400 militia and dockyard workers, 50 to 100 Indians) and its defences weak. These consisted of a few heavy guns mounted west of the town by the lakeshore. There was a small fort, but its only strong part was the stone magazine where ammunition was stored.

The American effort was big: 1,700 regulars carried on 14 ships led by the *Madison*. Chauncey commanded the fleet and Dearborn the troops. Shortly before dawn, the Americans landed west of the town where only a few Indians and regulars were present to oppose them. These defenders were easily driven back while American warships knocked out the shore batteries.

General Sheaffe, the British commander, soon realized he could not hold York. He advised the militia officers to surrender the town, and ordered the unfinished ship and the naval storehouse burned and the big magazine blown up. His intention was to destroy anything that could be of value to the Americans, but the explosion also caused them unexpected losses. The American commander on shore, Brigadier General Zebulon Pike was

Chauncey and his fleet approaching York on April 27, 1813.
[Reprinted from The War of 1812: The War For Canada, *by W.B. Turner (Toronto, Grolier Limited, 1982), p.43.]*

crushed by falling stones, 38 soldiers were killed and 22 wounded. Dearborn then came ashore to assume command.

Sheaffe and the regulars marched away, leaving the people, "standing in the street, like a parcel of sheep," in the words of York's sheriff, John Beikie.[3] Although the Americans had been angered by the magazine explosion (seeing it as an unfair trick), a surrender was negotiated, the militia were allowed to go to their homes and private property was to be left alone. Nevertheless, there was theft and destruction of property during the enemy's six-day occupation. Government House, the Parliament Building, other public buildings and a private schooner were all burned by the Americans. A number of private homes and stores were robbed.

In terms of the war, however, the most important consequences were the loss to the British of the badly needed naval and military stores, the ship under construction, and the *Duke of Gloucester*, which the Americans took away. The loss of supplies in particular contributed to the later, fatal, weakness of the Lake Erie squadron.

In January 1813, Chauncey had established a naval base at Presque Isle (now Erie, Pennsylvania), and several ships were soon under construction there. Captain Oliver H. Perry, a regular naval officer with experience of warfare at sea, was given command of the Lake Erie squadron. The British naval squadron on that lake was under Commander Robert H. Barclay. He too had experience of naval warfare, having lost an arm at the battle of Trafalgar.

The British position on Lake Erie was weaker than that of the Americans who could easily send seamen and equipment from Pittsburg and Philadelphia to Presque Isle. When British seamen arrived at Kingston in May, Yeo thought he needed most of them for Lake Ontario. He did not allow Barclay to take any to Lake Erie, even though there were not enough seamen on Erie to work the gunboats. Moreover, Barclay received insufficient guns and supplies to properly equip his ships.

Chauncey used his naval force again in May to support an American attack on Fort George. While he was away from Sackets Harbor, Prevost and Yeo attempted to capture it. During the assault, an American officer set fire to a schooner, a ship under construction and naval stores to keep them out of British hands. But an off-shore breeze kept Yeo's ships too far out for their guns to be effective. Deciding that the attack could not succeed, Prevost called it off. The Americans put out the fires before they had done much harm. Prevost thus failed to capture Sackets Harbor or even inflict much damage. He was later criticized for not pressing on with the attack.

Chauncey hurried back to his threatened base while Yeo sailed in the opposite direction, towards Burlington, carrying troops and supplies for the army which had been driven away from Fort George. Yeo used his ships to capture American supply boats and to cannonade the enemy on shore.

For the next two months the cautious Chauncey kept his fleet in Sackets Harbor because Yeo had a powerful new ship on the lake — the *Wolfe* (23 guns). To match it, the Americans built the *General Pike* (26 guns). When it was ready, Chauncey sailed out and headed for York. On July 31, the Americans again occupied the capital, seized supplies and burned storehouses.

During August, Yeo and Chauncey sailed near each other, but one or the other always thought conditions wrong for a real battle. The British ships had mostly short-range guns (carronades) and the Americans long-range guns. Yeo therefore wanted to get close to the Americans, while Chauncey wanted to fight at a distance when the water was calm. The result was that they never fought a decisive action.

Chauncey's force was weakened by the loss of two schooners, the *Hamilton* and the *Scourge,* which overturned in a storm and sank, taking most of their crewmen with them. Their approximate location in Lake Ontario was known but it would take years

O.H. Perry. A young naval officer with little experience of active
service, when he was sent to Lake Erie, Perry gained fame from his
victory there in September, 1813. But his naval service was cut short
when in 1819, at the age of 34, he died from yellow fever while on
active duty in South America.

[Courtesy of the Buffalo and Erie County Historical Society.]

of searching underwater before they would be located in 1975, just offshore from Port Dalhousie. Seven years later they would be thoroughly photographed and the results published.[4] In spring 1990, they would again be examined by a remote-controlled submersible and this time video images would be transmitted to audiences of scientists and school children. The pictures of the two vessels would show them resting upright on the lake bottom, containing a great deal of their original equipment and skeletal remains of the sailors, all remarkably well preserved by the ice cold water. Perhaps, someday, the plans to raise them and place them on a museum in Hamilton, Ontario, will be carried out. Then, instead of knowing only representations of warships from 1812-14, the public will be able to see two ships actually preserved from that era.

Aside from chasing each other, the two fleets did fight two brief battles in September, 1813. Yeo got the worst of both although in the second, he managed to inflict severe losses on the enemy. Nevertheless, Chauncey chased the British into Burlington Bay and after he sailed away, Yeo sought the safety of Kingston's harbour. Chauncey subsequently recaptured two schooners that Yeo had taken in August, and seized six ships carrying troops from York to Kingston.

Meanwhile, on Lake Erie, Perry had built a fleet within Presque Isle's sheltered harbour. But the large vessels (brigs) appeared to be trapped because they drew about three metres of water and there was less than two metres over the sand bar which lay across the entrance. Beyond the bar, Barclay's little fleet maintained a blockade until the end of July when it sailed away. During its absence until August 4, Perry had the brigs hauled over the barrier (the smaller ships were able to sail over it) and out on to the lake. The emergence of Perry's fleet created an immediate threat to Fort Malden and Procter's forces. In spite of the weaknesses of his fleet, Barclay had no choice but to fight Perry in order to eliminate the American naval menace.

On September 10, the two fleets approached each other among the Bass Islands near Put-in-Bay. Barclay had six ships, only three of them adequately armed, mostly with guns taken from Fort Malden. Perry had nine ships, all well armed with proper naval guns including some which could be swivelled around to shoot over either side. Firing began about noon and by mid-afternoon, Perry's flagship *Lawrence* (named after his

A Naval Battle on Lake Ontario: the United States sloop of war,
General Pike, and the British sloop of war, *Wolfe,* September 28, 1813.
[Courtesy of the Archives of Ontario, S1431.]

friend, the heroic Captain Lawrence) was "a floating helpless wreck."[5] Remarkably, Perry was unhurt and so transferred to his second large brig to continue the fight and by late afternoon, had defeated the British. The men on each side had fought bravely and had suffered terrible losses. Barclay, badly wounded in the thigh and his remaining arm, was taken prisoner along with all the other survivors. Perry now controlled Lake Erie, a result which would change the entire military situation for western Upper Canada.

During the final weeks of the navigation season, Chauncey pretty well controlled Lake Ontario. Nonetheless, regulars and militia going by bateaux from York made it safely to Kingston, one indication that Chauncey's evanescent control did not decisively affect the war. Yeo's fleet was secure in Kingston harbour and being made stronger for the next year's fighting. The two fleets, however, never again fought a battle.

On the other lakes that mattered to the defence, Champlain and Huron, the British retained control throughout 1813. In June, two American schooners sailed from Lake Champlain into the Richelieu River to stop smugglers taking supplies into Canada. They were trapped by British gunboats and surrendered. The British were now stronger on Champlain than the Americans. They used their superiority to destroy the defences at

Second View of Com. Perry's Victory. An overall view of the naval
engagement, suggesting a very orderly combat.
[Courtesy of the Buffalo and Erie County Historical Society.]

Plattsburg, seize military supplies at other places and capture
four small vessels. American farmers at least were pleased because they could still send foodstuffs to the British army.

WAR ALONG THE BORDER

Early in 1813, the United States decided to increase its efforts to
win the war. Congress approved a big war loan, appointed more
generals, asked President Madison to raise more troops, and
voted to build more ships. (This was why Chauncey and Perry
were able to undertake so much ship-building.) Madison
changed some of his cabinet members, one of his appointments
being John Armstrong as Secretary of War. Armstrong proved
more active than his predecessor, but his leadership and planning were no better. He left Dearborn in command of the
Northern Army until July, then replaced him with James Wilkinson, a man who was considered incompetent by many of his fel-
low officers. Wade Hampton, who was put in command of the
Lake Champlain front, was a better officer, but he and Wilkinson
hated each other. Armstrong blundered badly when he put these
two in charge of the most important land sector in the war.

Land warfare in 1813 began far to the west. Brigadier General James Winchester, another veteran of the American Revolution, was the new commander of part of the North Western
Army. The rest was under William Harrison, now a brigadier

Plaque at Fort York commemorating the Battle of York.
[Courtesy of the author.]

general, whose victory at Tippecanoe had won him the respect of many Americans. Harrison's aim was to recapture Detroit and then invade Upper Canada.

In January, Harrison led over 6,000 men north towards Detroit. Winchester went ahead with an advance guard and captured Frenchtown, but he took no precautions against a British counterattack. This came before dawn on January 22. Across the frozen river and through deep snow, Procter led over 500 regulars, militia and sailors. With the support of about 600 Indians, they captured some 500 Americans, including Winchester, and killed nearly 400 more. On hearing this, Harrison fled up the Maumee River. Finding that Procter did not pursue him, he returned downriver and built a fort which he named Fort Meigs after the governor of Ohio.

Procter was not the decisive leader that Brock had been. Instead of attacking while the Americans were building Fort Meigs, he waited for reinforcements. By the time they arrived in May, the fort was ready, and even with reinforcements Procter could not capture it. He ended the siege and returned to Amherstburg. Later in the year, he would try again, but his attacks achieved nothing worthwhile.

There had been fighting early in the year along the St. Lawrence River as well. American militia from Ogdensburg had several times raided across the river, threatening the supply route to Upper Canada. Ignoring Prevost's orders not to attack Ogdensburg, Lieutenant Colonel George Macdonell (known as "Red" George), the commander at Fort Wellington, decided to march against the American post in order to put an end to these raids. On February 22, British regulars and militia crossed the ice from Prescott. They captured the American guns, moved into the town, then attacked the strong fort nearby. The Americans withdrew, leaving the whole position in Macdonell's hands. He burned the barracks and boats before recrossing the river with supplies and prisoners.

For the rest of the war there was no garrison in Ogdensburg and therefore no need to fight there. In fact, people from Prescott occasionally went over to the American side to shop at David Parish's store, while Americans often crossed to have dinner with Macdonell. The inhabitants of this part of the frontier wanted to live in peace with each other, a feeling that was unfortunately not shared by most Americans.

CANADA INVADED

The Americans should have concentrated first along the St. Lawrence south of Montreal, but Armstrong did not think their forces would be ready early enough for such an attack. Instead, he planned to capture Kingston, which would give the Americans control of Lake Ontario. Then they would take York and afterwards, the British forts along the Niagara frontier. This was not a bad plan, but Armstrong changed it to a weaker one.

Reinforcements were arriving at Quebec and Prevost sent some of them, including the 104th Regiment, to Upper Canada.

A Private of the 8th (King's) Regiment of Foot, c. 1813. Toronto
Historical Board, Fort York.
[Courtesy of the author.]

In February, he went there himself to inspect the posts. All this
movement made Dearborn and Chauncey think the British were
too strong to be attacked successfully at Kingston. They proposed
the seizure of York to be followed by attacks along the Niagara

River. If all these assaults succeeded, they would then move against Kingston. Armstrong agreed to this new plan.

The Americans achieved the first part of their plan when they captured York in April. The next part, to take over the Niagara frontier, also succeeded, with Chauncey's fleet playing a major role.

On May 25, Chauncey's ships began to bombard Fort George and soon set its log buildings on fire. Two days later, between 4,000 and 5,000 Americans landed, led by Colonel Winfield Scott, a bold young regular officer who was Dearborn's chief of staff. Under heavy shell fire from the ships, Brigadier General John Vincent's defensive force of regulars and militia flank companies was unable to stop them. Vincent retreated to Beaver Dams up on the escarpment, where he had a supply depot in the farmhouse of John De Cew, a local settler. On Vincent's orders, all the troops from the rest of the Niagara frontier joined him.

Vincent sent the militia home and hurriedly retreated with his regulars, including two companies of the 8th Regiment just arrived from Kingston, to Burlington Bay. Here he had a strong position high above the lake yet beside a harbour and with land routes to both York and Amherstburg. The Americans now controlled the whole Niagara frontier, but their success was incomplete. They had not destroyed Vincent's army, which stood in the way of any further advance.

Dearborn ordered his forces to pursue the British. Meanwhile, Chauncey was heading back to Sackets Harbor and Yeo was sailing towards Burlington. On June 5, the American force of 3400 men camped in a field at Stoney Creek. With the escarpment on one side and a swamp on the other, they could only be attacked from the front. Guards were stationed ahead of the army, but they were few and not alert.

A local lad named Billy Green told the British of the American encampment and gave them the Americans' password. After scouting the enemy position, Lieutenant Colonel John Harvey persuaded Vincent to try a night attack. Through the darkness 704 men advanced silently towards the American sentries. Harvey had ordered them to take the flints out of their muskets so that they could not shoot and arouse the enemy. After silently bayoneting the American sentries, the troops rushed into the enemy's camp ... and started yelling!

The awakened Americans began to shoot, and a confused

struggle in the dark erupted. Men fired on troops of their own side. The American commanders blundered into British troops and were captured. Vincent became confused and got lost in the woods, not to be found until the next day by his men. The fighting ended before dawn with the British taking over 100 prisoners, including several officers.

Harvey collected his scattered troops and withdrew to his camp. The Americans retreated to 40 Mile Creek (Grimbsy), where they were reinforced by troops from the Niagara frontier. Still they were not safe. On June 7, Yeo's ships appeared and, inland, Canadian militia and Indians began to gather.

General Dearborn ordered a general retreat to Fort George. The Americans set fire to Fort Erie and withdrew from it and from Chippawa as well. Vincent moved forward, picking up supplies the Americans had left behind. Within a few days, he had troops posted at 20 Mile Creek (Jordan), 12 Mile Creek (St. Catharines) and De Cew's farmhouse. The Americans held onto the area from Fort George to Queenston.

Stoney Creek was a decisive battle, for it stopped the most threatening advance by the enemy into the Niagara Peninsula. The Americans would never again get as far into this vital part of Upper Canada. As well, the victory greatly boosted the morale of the defenders while causing dismay and confusion among the Americans.

Canada's defenders grew stronger. Vincent received more regulars and was able to send help to Procter at Amherstburg. Meanwhile, there had been growing criticism of Sheaffe's leadership, and for some weeks he had been too ill to perform his duties. Prevost removed him from the command of Upper Canada and put Major General Francis de Rottenburg in his place.

The invaders now held only a corner of the Peninsula. As a first step in breaking Vincent's defensive line, they decided to try to capture the post at De Cew's house. This was held by Lieutenant James FitzGibbon with about 50 men of the 49th Regiment; nearby, there were other troops, militia, and Indians.

Over 500 Americans with two guns marched up to Queenston on June 23 and spent the night there. The next day, in thick woods near Beaver Dams, they were ambushed by about 300 Indians from Lower Canada under Captain Dominique Ducharme of the Indian Department and 100 Mohawks led by Captain

Portrait bust of Laura Secord by Mildred Peel, O.S.A.
[In the collection of the Government of Ontario.]

William Kerr and John Brant. For some three hours the Americans fought desperately against attackers they could barely see. They were terrified that if they surrendered the Indians would kill them all. FitzGibbon heard the shooting and hurried over with his troops. By this time the Americans were more than willing to surrender to him. The victory, however, belonged to the Indians. FitzGibbon later wrote, "... not a shot was fired on our side by any but the Indians. They beat the American detachment into a state of terror ..."[6]

Beaver Dams was a small but important victory. American morale sank as, once again, a strong American force failed in a fairly simple task. The advance into Upper Canada was bringing not success but a series of humiliating defeats.

Col. Johnsons mounted men charging a party of British Artillerists and Indians, at the Battle fought near Moravian Town October 2nd 1813. when the whole of the British force commanded by Gen: Procter, surrendered to the Army under Gen. Harrison and his Gallant followers.

The Battle of Moravian Town, October 2, 1813.
[Courtesy of Lilly Library, Indiana University, Bloomington, Indiana.]

Beaver Dams was important to Canadians also because it produced the best known heroine of the war. Laura Secord overheard the American officers in Queenston talking about the plan to attack De Cew's house and thought no time should be lost in warning FitzGibbon. Although she had a farm, children and a wounded husband to look after, she undertook the difficult journey as soon as possible. Her route lay through thick woods, over sharp rocks and across unbridged streams with the additional danger that she might be caught by American patrols. Historians do not know for certain whether or not her mission affected the battle of Beaver Dams, but she deserves to be remembered for her loyalty and courage.

The situation on the Niagara front was now a stalemate. The Americans could not break out from Fort George and recapture the peninsula, but the British and Canadians could not retake the fort. Skirmishing continued. In July, regulars and militia twice raided American posts across the river, bringing back guns and supplies, including salt, which was scarce in Upper Canada. In August, there was a clash between the Indians on either side and an unsuccessful attack on Fort George. Basically, however, both sides had no choice but to settle down and wait the outcome of fighting elsewhere.

PROCTER'S DEFEAT AND THE DEATH OF TECUMSEH

American control of Lake Erie meant that even with Tecumseh's help Procter could not hold on to Detroit nor stay at Fort Malden and Amherstburg. Supplies were short and the supply line seriously endangered. He had fewer than 900 regulars (mostly of the 41st) all of whom were weary from fighting and weakened by fever. American forces numbering several thousand could easily surround his position. But Tecumseh, who wanted to stay and fight, vehemently opposed a retreat. Hence, relations between the two leaders became increasingly strained during the withdrawal and final battle.

Although Procter really had no choice but to retreat up the Thames River towards Vincent's army, his time-consuming preparations gave the Americans time to move their forces and follow close behind. Procter left Fort Malden on September 27, only hours before Harrison landed with his troops from Perry's ships. Reinforcements, including mounted riflemen, joined Harrison on October 1st. With his forces, now about 3,500 strong, he set out after Procter.

The British troops with their Indian allies, tired and hungry, struggled slowly over muddy trails in a badly organized retreat. No defences had been built so that troops could stop and fight delaying actions nor did Procter make sure that all the bridges were destroyed. The Americans, confident of victory, pursued quickly. By October 5, they were so close that Procter knew he had to make a stand. About three kilometres from Moraviantown, Procter turned to face the enemy. Fewer than 500 of his men were fit to fight. These he placed across the road and among trees with the river to their left. On their right, in a swamp, Tecumseh and about 800 Indians waited.

The battle was short and fierce. The American horsemen charged. The British troops, thrown into confusion, fired once or twice, then hastened to surrender. Procter tried valiantly to rally them but failed. He fled towards Moraviantown and beyond. Tecumseh and his Indians fought on bitterly until he was killed; then the survivors retreated.

Harrison burned Moraviantown, but decided not to advance further, probably because that would over-stretch his supply line. Once again, a serious American inroad into Upper Canada produced limited rather than decisive results. Harrison returned to Detroit where, on October 17, he issued a proclamation establishing civil administration for the Michigan Territory and western Upper Canada, thus beginning an occupation of the area that lasted for the remainder of the war.

During the days after the battle, Procter collected soldiers who had escaped and assembled 246 of them at Ancaster. Rottenburg, who was in Kingston, thought the setback so serious that everything west of Kingston should be abandoned. But Procter, Vincent and other officers at Burlington were determined to hold on to their position and changed his mind.

But it was different for many Indians, for with the death of Tecumseh they lost heart. They signed a cease-fire with Harrison and this ended organized Indian resistance to the Americans around Lake Erie. Further north, the Indians continued to support the British, who remained in control of the forts and lakes.

AMERICAN DEFEATS

By August, Armstrong realized that his plan was not achieving the conquest of Upper Canada. He wanted Kingston captured or cut off by an invasion down the St. Lawrence. Major General Wilkinson who had now taken over from Dearborn, agreed to try this in combination with a move against Montreal by Hampton.

In September, while preparations for the major attack were underway, Hampton tried to divert British attention by invading Lower Canada. He withdrew almost immediately — not because he was opposed, but because he could not find drinking water for his men and horses. His next attempt, further west along the route of the Chateauguay River, was no more successful. On October 21, he led about 3,000 soldiers with 10 guns into Lower Canada. Most of his New York militiamen, however, refused to cross the frontier.

In Hampton's way stood a force of 300 Canadian Fencibles, Canadian Voltigeurs, militia and a few Indians, all commanded by Lieutenant Colonel Charles de Salaberry. Behind them were about 1,200 militia and 150 Indians under Lieutenant Colonel Macdonell. Salaberry, from a prominent French-Canadian family, had served in the British army since 1793. (His father had served in the militia and three of his brothers were killed while fighting for the British). He had fought in the West Indies and Europe against the French. In the spring of 1812, Prevost appointed him to raise a Provincial Corps of Light Infantry, usually called the

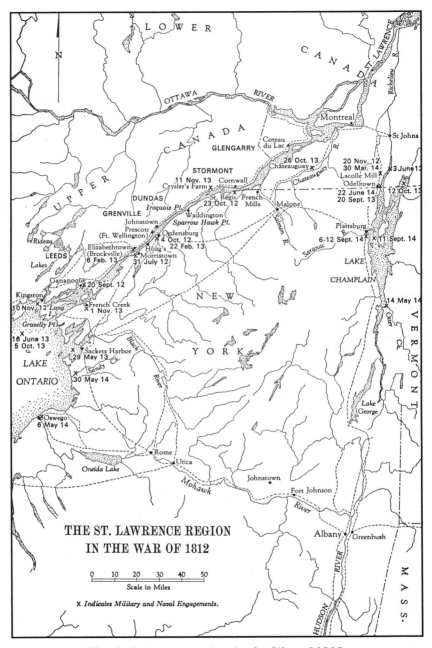

The St. Lawrence region in the War of 1812.
[Reprinted from The Defended Border *by Morris Zaslow,*
(Toronto, Macmillan of Canada, 1964), p. 64.]

A VIEW of WINCHESTER in NORTH AMERICA *DEDICATED* to Mʳ PRESIDENT MAD I SON!!

Cartoon depicting the European view of how the Indians treated and mocked prisoners of war.
[Courtesy of Lilly Library, Indiana University, Bloomington, Indiana.]

Canadian Voltigeurs. This was a militia corps and most of its recruits were Canadians from Lower Canada.

In a brief fight on October 25, Salaberry's few Canadians stopped Hampton's much larger force. Casualties were light: about 50 Americans to 25 Canadians. Yet the small battle of Chateauguay was important because it ended a serious threat to Montreal. Hampton retreated and soon withdrew to Lake Champlain for the winter. This battle is remembered also because it was won entirely by Canadians, both French- and English-speaking, fighting side by side. Chateauguay has become part of the Canadian sense of nationalism. Salaberry, who received a gold medal for the victory, became a Canadian hero.

Early in October, Wilkinson arrived at Sackets Harbor with all the regulars from the Niagara frontier. He decided not to attack Kingston because it had been reinforced. Instead, he set out with nearly 8,000 men and a large fleet of boats to advance down the St. Lawrence against Montreal. He did not know that Armstrong thought it was too late in the season for such an attack. In fact, Armstrong had decided the troops should go into winter quarters — but he had neglected to tell Wilkinson.

As soon as Rottenburg heard of the American advance, he ordered Lieutenant Colonel Joseph W. Morrison to pursue. Morrison's 630 regulars along with two small guns went on board two schooners. Reinforcements of 240 men joined him at Prescott. Bateaux carried supplies, and seven gunboats provided protection. The invaders employed hundreds of small boats to transport their men, horses, and guns all protected by 12 gunboats.

Wilkinson was not expecting any opposition as he advanced. To his surprise, Canadian militia hurried to the riverbank and, hiding behind trees and rocks, took every opportunity to shoot at the invaders. Wilkinson had to land 2,500 soldiers on the Canadian side to drive them away and to protect his boats as they passed through the Long Sault rapids. Learning about the forces pursuing him, he sent another 2,000 regulars to act as a rear guard. This unit alone outnumbered the pursuers.

On the night of November 10, Wilkinson set up his headquarters in Michael Cook's tavern. Less than two kilometres away, Morrison was spending the night in the home of John Crysler, a prosperous farmer and captain in the Dundas militia. Outside, cold rain and sleet fell upon the soldiers of both armies as they tried to sleep on the ground.

Early next morning, Indians fired on an American scouting party. Each side thought the other was attacking. Wilkinson ordered his rear guard to drive the British away. Disregarding sniping by Indians and Voltigeurs in the woods and cannon fire from British gunboats, the Americans attacked. Steady musket volleys from the British 8th and 49th Regiments stopped them in their tracks. When the British charged, supported by deadly artillery fire, the Americans fled the field. Two days later, an American soldier wrote in a letter "Our troops retreated with great precipitation to the boats, and crossed the river, leaving the British on the field .... What appears most extraordinary in this affair is that nearly 1,000 of our troops crossed to the American side during the engagement"[7] — which appears to mean they deserted under fire!

Despite this defeat, Wilkinson's force was still the stronger by far, and on November 12, the Americans passed the rapids. But Wilkinson was sick, his morale as well as the army's was low, and winter was coming. The invaders realized that they had a long way to go to Montreal and that capturing it would be far from easy.

Wilkinson and Hampton acting together could have cut the route from Montreal to Upper Canada. Any hope of this out-

Contemporary British cartoon mocking American sea power.
[Courtesy of Lilly Library, Indiana University, Bloomington, Indiana.]

come ended with Hampton's withdrawal to Lake Champlain and when Wilkinson got the news, he was furious. Blaming Hampton for the failure of the invasion, he took his army out of Canada. It was the ignominious end of the major American effort against Montreal during the entire war.

Although the offensive against Montreal failed, it did affect events in the Niagara Peninsula. Very few American regulars were left along the Niagara frontier. All the posts, including Fort George, were occupied by a few hundred New York militia under the command of Brigadier General George McClure, a militia officer. The British managed to retake the smaller posts one by one, and by December the Americans held only the fort.

The American militia's term of service was nearing its end. They began to return to their homes, leaving McClure with no more than 100 men. Hearing that Colonel John Murray was advancing with a small force, McClure decided to abandon Fort George. Before doing so, he gave an order which would disgrace the American forces and lead to much suffering along the frontier.

Back in October, Armstrong had given McClure authority to destroy Newark if necessary for the defence of Fort George. There was now no reason for McClure to do so, since he was abandoning the fort. Yet on the night of December 10, he ordered the town burned. About 400 people were forced out of their homes to stand in the cold and snow while the fires were set. Then the Americans crossed the river to Fort Niagara.

Murray's force reached Newark that night. William H. Merritt who was with him, wrote, "Nothing but heaps of coals and the streets full of furniture that the inhabitants were fortunate enough to get out of their houses, met the eye in all directions. Mr. Gordon's house ... was the only one standing."[8]

This wanton destruction made many Canadians bitter. They wanted revenge and were not appeased by the American government's statement that McClure's action was unauthorized. Nor was McClure's claim that he merely intended to deny winter quarters to the British forces convincing. He had, after all, left tents behind as well as the buildings of Fort George. In fact, the fort was in better condition than when the British had lost it.

On December 16, Lieutenant General Gordon Drummond arrived at Fort George and took over civil and military authority from Rottenburg, who went to Lower Canada to take command of the defences there. Born in Quebec in 1771, Drummond had served the British army in Europe, the West Indies, Egypt and Canada, where, in 1813, he had been made second in command to Prevost. This young, determined and ambitious Lieutenant General was accompanied by Major General Phineas Riall. He replaced Vincent who was ill, while Sheaffe returned to England and Procter, in disgrace because of his defeat in October, was given the unimportant job of command at York.

Murray and Drummond immediately planned an attack on Fort Niagara. McClure, on the other side, feared such an assault and retreated to Buffalo leaving just over 400 men in the fort but their officers apparently enjoyed too much the distractions of gambling and drinking. The British brought boats from Burlington and the militia helped to drag them overland to the river above Fort George. Despite the snow and severe cold, over 500 men under Murray crossed the river on the night of December 18. In the darkness of early morning they suprised the guards and forced their way through the main gate. The startled Americans — many still in their beds — put up only a brief fight.

Murray's capture of Fort Niagara was an important gain for the British. They took nearly 350 prisoners and great quantities of military supplies, clothing (including thousands of pairs of

"The Burning of Buffalo"
[Courtesy of the Buffalo and Erie County Historical Society.]

shoes!) and blankets. They now commanded the western end of Lake Ontario, which meant that Chauncey could not use his ships to supply troops along that frontier. This would affect later campaigns. Also, the British now held American territory and would keep it for the rest of the war.

Riall, with a reserve force of regulars and Indians under Colonel Matthew Elliott (who was about 74 years old), crossed the next day to support Murray. Since his help was not needed, he advanced on Lewiston, where American guns threatened Queenston. Most of the inhabitants fled. Riall destroyed Lewiston and a few other small settlements. This was the beginning of the retaliation for the burning of Newark.

A call went out for militia to defend Buffalo, and McClure was replaced. But these preparations proved completely inadequate. Leading some 1500 troops and several hundred Indians, Riall crossed the river from Chippawa on the night of December 29. He captured Black Rock and Buffalo, took supplies and then burned those villages as well as four armed vessels. The American commander wrote to the Governor of New York lamenting, "The flourishing village of Buffalo is laid in ruins. The Niagara frontier now lies open and naked to our enemies."[9]

The year 1813 had seen the British in North America lose battles, territory and control of Lake Erie, yet the Americans seemed no closer to victory because several major invasion efforts into Canada had failed. In light of those setbacks and of Napoleon's defeats in Europe, the Americans could not be confident of winning the war in the year to come.

LIFE OF THE PEOPLE

The people of Canada, especially Upper Canada, were more affected by the war in 1813 than they had been in 1812. Along the St. Lawrence, at York, and all through the Niagara Peninsula and the Western District, homes, businesses and crops were destroyed.

Out of 625 people in York, twenty-two later asked the government to compensate them for losses suffered during the American occupation. According to their claims, the Americans had helped themselves to everything from kitchen tools, bedding and clothing to silverware, books and medical instruments. Ely Playter hid in the woods when the Americans came to his farm house on Yonge Street and watched helplessly as they took his sword, razors, powder horn, shot pouch, jewellry and clothing. W.W.Baldwin sent his silverware to be hidden in a friend's barn out of town before the invaders arrived. Those who stayed in their homes were not molested by the Americans who looted empty houses, but several store owners suffered losses even though they were present.

The Americans gave some of the articles they took to Canadians in the town, possibly in the hope of winning their support. This was probably why the magistrates issued a warning on April 30 reminding the townspeople that it was treason to aid the enemy.

The problems of lawlessness and disloyalty were even greater in the Niagara Peninsula and western Upper Canada. American troops encouraged any residents willing to aid them. Farms were looted not only by Americans but by a few traitors as well. The most notorious of these was Joseph Willcocks, who had come from Ireland to Upper Canada about 1800. When he went over to the Americans, Willcocks formed a corps called the Canadian Volunteers. They rode about the Niagara Peninsula doing whatever they could to help the Americans. Two other prominent men who deserted to the invaders were Abraham Markle and Benajah Mallory. Both, like Willcocks, had once been members of the Upper Canada assembly.

These men and others like them may have had good reasons for discontent with the government of Upper Canada, but their conduct during the war was dishonourable. They tried to weaken the province's defences by encouraging others to desert and by capturing militia officers and supplies. They plundered and destroyed property and harmed people who had been their neighbours.

In November, a band of renegades including Mallory was surprised by a group of Norfolk militia in a house near Port Dover. Several were killed in the fight that followed, some escaped, and eighteen were taken prisoner. Four would be hanged in 1814 for treason. Unfortunately, the militia were not usually this successful in protecting people and preventing raids. Many peaceful farmers in the Western District suffered, and their troubles would increase in 1814.

There appears to have been no problem of traitors in Lower Canada or the Maritime provinces. People there who may have favoured the American cause did not have American troops to support them. If they did not leave the provinces, they kept quiet.

The increased amount of fighting on Canadian soil had other direct effects on the people. Every battle left dead and wounded to be taken care of. The British army had medical men but never enough. Civilians usually had to help. Militiamen had to be looked after by their families. This meant that many families had the burdens of caring for a wounded man as well as those of working the farm. The Secords in Queenston are an example. If a man was killed or taken prisoner, the family had to carry on, perhaps with some financial help from the Loyal and Patriotic Society and the government.

The arrival of more and more soldiers and sailors in Canada, meant more sales of food, hay for horses, and wood for buildings and ships. The farmers, merchants, and workers of Upper Canada benefitted. Those who owned wagons and horses or oxen to pull them also were given plenty of employment.

Yet, these economic gains were more than offset by the increasing strains that the war imposed on the inhabitants' patience, courage and loyalty. At times, the government did not have the cash to pay for supplies it purchased. Payment was promised ... sometime in the future. This could mean a wait of months or even years. As late as March 1814, some farmers had still not been paid for supplies sold in 1812. Meanwhile, these people had to make their living and pay their bills. Militiamen, and occasionally soldiers, were not always paid on time either.

Shortages of pay, food and clothing increased discontent among the militia. Even the most loyal citizen could not devote all his time to militia duty. In May, Prevost reported some militiamen deserting not because they were disloyal but because they wanted to return to their farms to plant crops. Militiamen in the Western and Niagara Districts also gave their parole to the Americans. This meant that they promised not to fight; in a sense they were regarded as prisoners of war even though they continued to live at home. Some men willingly gave their parole perhaps because they were pro-American or perhaps simply to avoid being killed or injured. In September, Prevost warned against this practice and threatened to send these people to the United States.

The first use of martial law also showed the increasing strain of the war. When Procter found farmers refusing to sell him produce for the troops, he proclaimed partial martial law. This meant that the people came under military law and were required to sell supplies to the army. At different times, Prevost authorized Sheaffe and Rottenburg to impose martial law but neither acted until November when the latter proclaimed martial law in the Eastern and Johnstown Districts (along the St. Lawrence) in order to force farmers to sell him supplies. The Assembly subsequently passed a resolution protesting that "arbitrary and unconstitutional measure."[10]

The government's use of martial law did not mean it wanted to destroy the people's freedom. Nor did it mean the people were in rebellion against the government. What it shows is that the British commanders were worried and very nervous. They feared they would lose the province. It also shows that the ordinary people were not warlike. They were weary of warfare and wanted to return to normal, peaceful life. In spite of the defeat of two major American invasions, in spite of the good service by the militia, 1813 ended unhappily.

4
CHECKS AND STALEMATES, 1814

For the British and their allies, 1814 began with the prospect of hard fighting ahead in France, but with the strong possibility that Napoleon would finally be defeated. He had almost reached the limits of French manpower, whereas the already powerful forces against him were gaining in strength. In spite of the burdens of war in Europe, Britain was now able to give more attention to the struggle in America. Although the European situation was improving, the British government had no wish to continue the war with the United States. In November 1813, Foreign Secretary Lord Castlereagh had sent a letter to President Madison suggesting peace negotiations. The message had arrived in the United States on December 30 along with the news of Napoleon's defeat at Leipzig. Fearing that the British would soon be able to send massive land and naval forces to North America, Madison was eager to seek peace. In January 1814, Congress agreed to his proposal to negotiate, and delegates were sent to Europe.

The war against Napoleon entered its final stage as allied armies invaded France itself. From the north came German,

Austrian, Prussian and other troops, Wellington's army broke in from Spain to the south and an Austrian force threatened to attack from Italy in the east. Napoleon still won battles, but he was steadily losing the war. On March 31, the allies captured Paris. Soon afterwards, Napoleon gave up.

After April, therefore, the British navy was freed from fighting duties in Europe. Fewer troops were needed there, and reinforcements and supplies could be sent across the Atlantic. By July, the government would send to Canada fourteen regiments of Wellington's veterans along with several experienced generals.

Soon afterwards, the British-American negotiations would begin in earnest and each side would make tough demands on the other, each wanting to gain as much as it could from the peace treaty. As a result, the months would pass while the delegates talked. Meanwhile, many fierce battles would be fought on land and water. And the British position would grow stronger.

PREPARATIONS FOR WAR IN 1814

As the third year of the war opened, the American government's planning continued to display confusion. In February, Armstrong proposed an attack on Kingston along with a pretended invasion across the Niagara River. But Chauncey and Major General Jacob Brown, the commander of the land forces at Sackets Harbor, still thought their forces too weak to attack Kingston. Brown therefore marched most of the troops to the Niagara frontier. Then he changed his mind and hurried back to Sackets Harbor, leaving the troops behind.

In the spring, the American government revised its strategy for a number of reasons. First, the route to Montreal seemed to be too strongly defended. This was shown by the failure of Wilkinson's invasion. On March 30, he crossed the border with 4,000 men and seized Odelltown, north of Lake Champlain. A few kilometres further, he came up to a stone-walled mill at Lacolle defended by a small number of British regulars, marines, and Lower Canadian militia (including Voltigeurs). When he found that his guns inflicted no damage on the mill, he quickly broke off his attack and retreated across the border. This ended his unimpressive military career; he was replaced by Major General George Izard. Second, the Americans could not attack on

Lake Ontario because the British achieved superiority there by launching two new frigates in April. The next month, Yeo and Drummond attacked Oswego, capturing supplies and weapons. Yeo then used his ships to blockade Sackets Harbor to prevent the Americans bringing guns and other equipment for the ships under construction there.

By this time, with Napoleon's defeat in Europe, the Americans knew that large British reinforcements would soon be on the way to Canada. They had to act quickly and in an area where they did have superiority. They therefore decided the main attack should go across the Niagara against Fort Erie. If Brown captured it, he was to advance against Burlington and then York. Yet the tendency to disperse forces rather than concentrating them against the main objective was shown when the cabinet decided to send troops from Detroit against Michilimackinac instead of taking Armstrong's advice to shift them to Brown's army on the Niagara.

The plan to capture the Niagara Peninsula rested on American control of Lake Erie and Chauncey's promise to have his fleet out on Lake Ontario early in July. He expected to have two ships ready by then, which would give him superiority over Yeo's fleet. Yet even if all these American plans succeeded, they would not achieve a decisive victory in the war. For that objective the best strategy would still have been to cut the St. Lawrence route.

The British government followed a simple and sensible strategy, perhaps because it could not do much else. It sought to defend Canada by sending more soldiers, sailors and supplies. Prevost and Drummond were determined to hold on to Fort Niagara and to improve defences along the frontier. To this end they built a small fort on the Lake Ontario shore near Fort George, calling it Fort Mississauga, and another on top of Queenston Heights, calling it Fort Drummond. Finally, the government planned attacks on the United States so that Britain would be in a stronger position when the final peace settlement was made.

The early months of 1814 saw little fighting along the border. The Americans were busy making plans and trying to collect, organize and train troops. In Canada, both Prevost and Drummond were occupied with political matters in their legislatures until March. As well, they were waiting for reinforcements and supplies from Britain.

Until July, the main events were raids rather than battles. In February, troops and militia raided American posts across the St. Lawrence. On May 30, Commander Stephen Popham led nearly 200 sailors and marines up Sandy Creek (near Sackets Harbor) to attack American boats taking guns and other ships' supplies to Chauncey. However, the Americans had a stronger force, including Indians. They ambushed Popham, forcing him to surrender. The loss of these men to Yeo was serious, for he could not quickly replace experienced seamen. The American supplies got through, Chauncey was able to complete his shipbuilding, and so Yeo ended his blockade.

Further west, the Americans took the initiative because they controlled Lake Erie. They were most successful in rapid hit-and-run raids along the shores of the lake. In May, about 800 of them landed at Port Dover and burned every building from there to Turkey Point. The Canadian Volunteers took part in this and other raids during the summer. Several of these raids were directed against Port Talbot. The Canadian traitors wanted to capture Colonel Thomas Talbot, who had founded the Talbot Settlement and whose strict control over the settlers had made some of them hate him. He was also commander of the first Regiment of the Middlesex Militia. Port Talbot was raided in May, July, August, and September. In the August raid, Talbot narrowly escaped capture by running out one door of his house as the raiders came in the other.

The raids continued through the summer and autumn. Homes were robbed, houses, barns and even crops were burned. Some people were murdered and others taken prisoner. It was a nasty kind of warfare made worse by traitors taking revenge against former neighbours.

CANADA INVADED

By the beginning of July, Major General Brown had over 3,500 troops, mainly regulars, and about 600 Indians. Most of the troops were in two brigades, one under Brigadier General Winfield Scott, the other under Brigadier General Eleazar Ripley. To defend the entire frontier, Major General Riall had fewer than 2,500 men. Brown aimed his attack at the defenders' weakest point, Fort Erie.

Early on the morning of July 3, the Americans landed on both sides of the fort. By 5 p.m. they had forced its garrison of less than 150 men to surrender. The next day, the Americans advanced towards Chippawa with Scott's brigade in front. They found a strong British force on the opposite side of the Chippawa (Welland) River and so retreated a short way until the rest of the army caught up.

The British force they saw was commanded by Riall who had hurried there from Fort George and ordered reinforcements to follow. By July 5, he had about 1,500 regulars and 300 militia and Indians at Chippawa.

South of the river, American militia and Indian allies skirmished with Canadian militia and Indian allies. Then Riall, instead of staying in his strong defensive position, crossed the river and attacked the invaders. He thought the American army was smaller than it was and that it could not stand up to veteran British regulars. These American troops, however, were better trained and led than any that had previously invaded Canada. When he saw how professionally they marched and manoeuvred, Riall is supposed to have exclaimed, "'Those are regulars, by God!'"[1] In the battle of Chippawa, the British suffered heavy losses and had to withdraw across the river. Two days later Riall was forced to move back still farther as the Americans crossed the river, advanced to Queenston and occupied it. But the British still held all the rest of the peninsula and Drummond was coming with reinforcements.

From the small area of the peninsula they held, the Americans sent out scouting and raiding parties. There were skirmishes between them and regulars, militia, and Indians. Merritt, who took part in this fighting, wrote in his journal, "The militia were daily skirmishing and driving in the States' parties, who were plundering every house they could get at: they even plundered women of everything they had."[2] On July 18 there was a clash near the village of St. Davids; the next day, American troops burned it to the ground. When General Brown heard of this, he dismissed the militia officer responsible, thus indicating that men under his command would be required in future to act more responsibly towards civilians.

Brown expected Chauncey's ships to bring him supplies and to support his attacks on the British-held forts. But Chauncey feared for the safety of Sackets Harbor, even though he now had two new ships which made his fleet more powerful then Yeo's. As days passed and no help arrived, with his army declining in strength, Brown felt increasingly insecure at the end of a long and exposed supply line. On July 24, he withdrew to Chippawa. Riall decided to follow Brown and so, that night, sent 1,000 regulars under Lieutenant Colonel Thomas Pearson up the Portage Road. The next day, Riall led the rest of his troops in the same direction and soon after, came Drummond leading the 89th Regiment. They were heading towards a hill on Lundy's Lane where it crossed the Portage Road.

When Brown heard about the British advance, he changed his plans. He sent Scott with his brigade back to retake Queenston and prepared to follow with the rest of the army. They would march north along the Portage Road and so meet the British at Lundy's Lane. The outcome of these converging movements was the battle at Lundy's Lane which for several reasons, was both a confused and a prolonged action. The American army advanced in parts with Scott's brigade well ahead. Sections of the British forces were retreating and others advancing because their commanders were not sure of the size of the invading army. Furthermore, the struggle lasted from about 6 p.m. until midnight which meant that much of it was fought in the dark, illuminated only by the flashes of guns and muskets.

As the Americans advanced, Riall ordered Pearson to withdraw from Lundy's Lane. He thought Brown's whole army was attacking and did not know that Drummond was coming to his support. When Drummond arrived at the hill, he saw the American attack developing and immediately recognized that whoever possessed that high ground would have the advantage. He stopped the withdrawal and sent orders to other detachments to hurry to Lundy's Lane. The key of the position was the hill where British artillery was placed to fire at any advancing force. The Americans tried to take the guns by assaulting the flanks as well as the front. Scott's men almost succeeded in getting around the left flank but were driven back after capturing Riall, who had been seriously wounded. The Americans were not strong enough to advance again until the rest of their army arrived.

First Regiment of Foot (The Royal Scots) was sometimes referred to as "Pontius Pilate's Bodyguards" because it was the most senior regular regiment of the British army. The first battalion arrived at Quebec in August, 1812 and served at various posts in Lower Canada. In 1813, the men fought at Sackets Harbor, Fort Niagara, and Black Rock and in 1814 at Longwoods, Chippawa, Lundy's Lane, the seige of "Niagara" on its colours. The 4th battalion served at Quebec from June 1814 until July 1815.

[Courtesy of Canadian Park Service.]

Brown renewed the attack, and a small detachment captured the British guns. They were soon forced back by British troops attacking with bayonets. The fighting raged back and forth on the hill, neither side able to gain complete control. Dead and wounded soldiers lay where they had fallen on the battlefield. Still the living continued to battle though the light was fading. At some time after 9 o'clock, Colonel Hercules Scott arrived with 1,200 men to reinforce the British line. The British soldiers charged and beat off American attacks. Brown and Winfield Scott were both wounded and withdrew from the battle. Drummond, though wounded in the neck, continued to command. Finally, just before midnight, Brown ordered his exhausted army to retreat to Chippawa. The British troops and Canadian militia were too weary to do anything but fall asleep on the battlefield.

Losses were heavy on both sides. Over 700 Americans and 600 British were killed or wounded, making Lundy's Lane the bloodiest battle of the war. It was also a turning point: Brown's advance into Upper Canada was stopped. This was the last invasion of the province.

Neither side can be said to have won the battle (although Brown later claimed he did), but it was the Americans who retreated and who acted like a beaten force. They threw baggage, camp equipment and provisions into the Niagara River, burned Street's Mills, and destroyed the bridge over the Chippawa. Ripley wanted to withdraw all the way to Buffalo, but Brown insisted on holding onto Fort Erie.

When the Americans had captured the fort, it had only three guns and was open in the rear. It was too weak to be held against a determined attack. Brigadier General Edmund P. Gaines, who had replaced Brown, set engineers to work to make it stronger. They made a dry ditch and an earth wall right around the rear of the fort. These were covered by guns placed on newly built bastions. By early August, the Americans had about 2,200 troops inside this large and now well fortified camp.

After the battle at Lundy's Lane, Drummond did not pursue the Americans. He gave his troops time to recover and waited for reinforcements. Yet, there is a strong possibility that if he had advanced quickly to Fort Erie, even a small force might have driven the Americans across the river. In the last days of July, the British might have captured the fort as easily as the Americans had on the third.

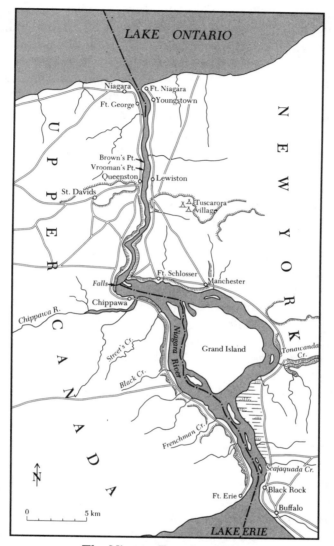

LAKE ONTARIO

NEW YORK

UPPER CANADA

The Niagara Frontier, 1812
[Reprinted from The War of 1812: Land Operations, *by George F. G. Stanley (Toronto, Macmillan of Canada, 1983), p. 123.]*

Early in August, Drummond prepared to besiege Fort Erie. While big guns were being brought from Fort George to blast the defensive works, he camped outside the fort with over 3,000 regulars to prevent the Americans from advancing inland. The actual attack on the fort began on August 15, after a bombardment which had begun two days previously. Just after 2 a.m., British columns assaulted the fort in three places.

The largest column (over 1000 men) attacked the south end but suffered many casualties without achieving anything. The other two columns were met at the north end by heavy cannon and musket fire. After severe losses the survivors of the two columns joined forces, and together they penetrated the northeast bastion. The fighting raged fiercely as the British tried to push into the fort itself. The American defenders were soon reinforced by troops no longer needed at the south end. Drummond, too, sent reinforcements from his reserve, but most were stopped by American gunfire.

Suddenly, a large store of gunpowder under the bastion exploded, killing many of the attackers and blowing others into the ditch. Few were unhurt. Most of the defenders were behind barracks which protected them from the blast. The British attack ended ignominiously, as the troops fled back to their camp north of Fort Erie.

The sun rose to reveal heaps of dead and wounded men in the ditch and along the lakeshore. British losses were 366 killed or wounded and 539 missing, many of them prisoners. American casualties numbered only 84 in total. The severity of British losses is illustrated by Dr. William Dunlop's description of the effect on his regiment: "After the blow up, our little corps was broken up, and the companies composing it joined their respective battalions. My own regiment was wretchedly reduced; little more than three months before it had gone into the Battle of the Falls, five hundred strong, with a full complement of officers. Now we retired about sixty rank and file, commanded by a Captain, two of the senior Lieutenants carrying the colours, and myself marching in the rear—voilà, His Majesty's 89th Regiment of Foot!"[3]

Why did the night attack fail? For one thing, Drummond's bombardment had not sufficiently damaged the fort's defences. But the main reason was that the Americans were prepared. As soon as the British guns stopped firing, Gaines and Ripley put their men on the alert. Without the advantage of surprise, the British attack could not succeed against strong defences manned by steady troops under good leaders.

Drummond continued the siege but could not capture the fort. On the other hand, the Americans could not break out or advance. They could do little except suffer casualties in reply to the merciless bombardment from the British

The Battle of Lundy's Lane produced the heaviest losses of the war.
Both sides claimed victory, but it was the Americans who retreated.
[Reprinted from The War of 1812: The War For Canada, *by W.B. Turner
(Toronto, Grolier Limited, 1982), p.65.]*

siege batteries. One hundred and seventy-three years later, the
bones of at least 28 men who died during those weeks were discovered at Snake Hill on Lake Erie. That position, anchoring the
extreme western end of the defences of Fort Erie, had included
a hospital cemetery. The soldiers' remains — carefully uncovered
during the winter of 1987-88 — showed signs not only of wounds
(predominantly on the left side) but also of disease and stress
caused probably by heavy work and long marches. (The remains
were given military honours when they were reburied at Bath
National Cemetery, New York, on July 1, 1988.)

By mid-September Drummond was becoming discouraged.
Perry controlled Lake Erie while Chauncey had come out on to
Ontario and was blockading Fort George, which prevented supplies from reaching the army. More and more of Drummond's
troops were falling sick and all were miserable because of constant rain. General Brown, after he resumed command of the
American forces, launched a sortie against three new batteries
that Drummond was building to bombard Fort Erie. Catching
the British by surprise, the Americans put two of the batteries
out of commission before being driven back to the fort. Soon
after this severe setback, on September 21, Drummond ended
the siege. He placed his guns in strong positions along the
Chippawa River, and withdrew most of his troops to Chippawa
and Fort George.

The American commander, unable to advance inland from Fort Erie and knowing that command of Lake Ontario had switched to the British, decided to end the futile campaign. On November 5, he withdrew from the fort and then blew it up.

Thus, at the end of 1814 as at the beginning, the Americans held no Canadian territory along the Niagara; the British held Fort Niagara but could not advance any farther.

STALEMATE

During 1814, developments in other areas reflected those in the Niagara Peninsula. By the end of the year, along the Canadian border, neither side had gained new territory or lost what they had held at the beginning.

THE NORTHWEST

In the Northwest, the Americans tried to capture British posts in order to destroy the British-Indian alliance, which had continued despite the American capture of Detroit. This strategy was advanced when, in June, an American force seized Prairie du Chien, a fur-trading post on the Mississippi River. The next month, Lieutenant Colonel George Croghan sailed from Detroit with over 700 men to attack Michilimackinac. But Prevost had reinforced that post.

Lieutenant Colonel Robert McDouall had arrived at Michilimackinac with troops and supplies on May 18. When he learned of the American capture of Prairie du Chien, McDouall knew he would have to retake the post to keep Indian support. He sent William McKay, a fur trader, with a force of militia, traders, Indians and one regular artilleryman with a small gun. McKay found the Americans had built a fort (Fort Shelby), but after a three-day siege, the Americans surrendered. When Croghan landed on the Island on August 4, McDouall was ready for him. Fighting outside the fort with his regulars, Indians and militia, he defeated the larger American force, which retreated to its boats. The next day, Croghan departed leaving the schooners *Tigress* and *Scorpion* behind to blockade Michilimackinac.

On his way back to Detroit, Croghan discovered the British schooner *Nancy* hidden on the Nottawasaga River. This North

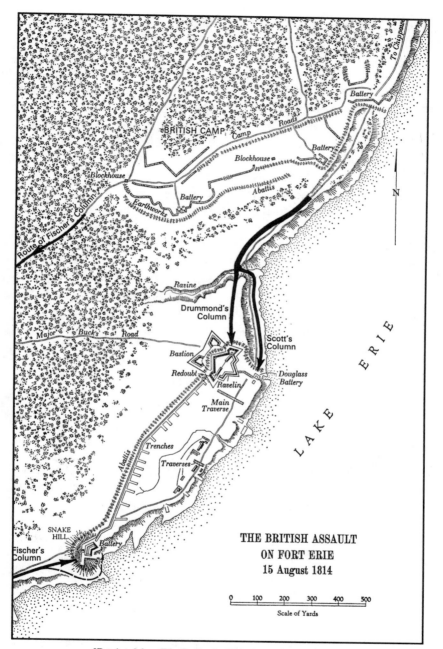

THE BRITISH ASSAULT
ON FORT ERIE
15 August 1814

Scale of Yards

[Reprinted from The Defended Border *by Morris Zaslow,*
(Toronto, Macmillan of Canada, 1964), p. 157.]

West Company vessel had been taken over by the British government for use as a transport on Lakes Erie and Huron. Croghan knew that if he destroyed the *Nancy*, the British would have great difficulty getting supplies to Michilimackinac. Lieutenant Miller Worsley, who commanded the British force, set fire to the schooner to prevent her capture.

The Americans now had the only sailing vessels on Lake Huron, but their superior position did not last long. Worsley and his men paddled canoes all the way from the Nottawasaga to Michilimackinac. On September 3, Worsley set out at night with 92 men in row-boats to attack the *Tigress*. The Americans spotted them and began shooting, but the Indians and British managed to clamber aboard the schooner and capture it.

Two days later, Worsley sailed the *Tigress* towards the *Scorpion*, craftily keeping the American flag flying and his soldiers hidden. When he was close enough, he fired the *Tigress*'s cannon. The Americans were taken completely by surprise and the British had little trouble seizing the *Scorpion*.

The two captured ships restored British naval dominance on Lake Huron. They retained it, the fort at Michilimackinac, and Indian support for the rest of the war. But they could not drive the Americans out of the western part of Upper Canada or recapture Detroit.

CHECK ON THE LAKES

On Lake Ontario, after Chauncey came out in August, Yeo remained in port until his new ship was ready. The *St. Lawrence*, launched on September 10, swung the balance of power to the British. It was a huge three-decker, designed to carry 112 guns and at least 700 crewmen. Chauncey withdrew to Sackets Harbor and Yeo came out on the lake on October 15.

The shipbuilding race continued. The Americans and the British started three new ships each. The only one to be launched before the end of the war was the British frigate *Psyche*. The frames for this vessel had been built in Britain and transported to Canada where it was assembled. American shipbuilders would now have to compete not only with Kingston but also with British shipyards. This change, which threatened to give Canada's defence a significant advantage, did not last long, for the shipbuilding contest was coming to an end.

To create his fleet on Lake Ontario, Yeo made sure that most naval supplies and seamen arriving in Canada were sent to Kingston. As a result, little help could be sent to Ile aux Noix, the British naval base on Lake Champlain. Superiority on this lake had swung to the Americans, and, in response, the British were building a frigate to strengthen their fleet.

The frigate was launched late in August and a new British commander, Captain George Downie, was sent to Lake Champlain. When he arrived there on September 2, he faced the difficult task of getting the new ship ready for service in a few days.

An attack on Plattsburgh had been planned earlier in the year as part of the British aim to be in a strong position for the peace negotiations. The government provided over 13,000 troops from Europe, most of whom had served under Wellington. On September 1, Prevost led an army 10,351 strong across the border, the most powerful British army seen along the frontier during the entire war.

On the 6th, Prevost halted on the north side of the Saranac River across from Plattsburgh. On the other side, about 3000 troops worked hard to strengthen the fortifications while militiamen of New York and Vermont flocked in and skirmished with the British along the river. Nearby, in Plattsburgh Bay, Captain Thomas Macdonough's squadron of four ships and ten gunboats lay at anchor. Prevost decided to wait for Captain Downie to arrive with his fleet so that the army and navy could attack at the same time. Every day he wrote Downie urging him to hurry his ships down to Plattsburgh. The Captain did not dare attack without his new frigate. He was still making up crews for his vessels as late as September 9, and the frigate was not completely finished when it sailed with the squadron before dawn on the eleventh.

The British and American fleets began battling between 8 and 9 a.m. Only minutes later, Downie was killed but the fierce fight continued for two hours. Then the British, who had suffered great losses, gave up.

Prevost did not launch his assault on the American land defences when the naval battle began. He ordered Major General Frederick P. Robinson to start the attack at 10 a.m. An hour or so later, most of the troops had crossed the Saranac and were forming up to charge the American positions. Robinson and his troops, veterans of battles against tough French soldiers, re- garded the American positions as an easy target. Their self-con- fidence was never put to the test, however, because Prevost halted the land attack as soon as Downie's fleet surrendered. He or- dered the troops to destroy their extra supplies and retreat. The army arrived back in Canada virtually unharmed.

The entire Plattsburgh campaign had failed, achieving nothing except the destruction of the British naval force on Lake Champlain. The situation was a stalemate. British army strength still blocked the Americans from invading Lower Canada; American control of Lake Champlain still prevented the British from occupying American territory in the area. Nonetheless, the battle of Plattsburgh was important for its effect on the peace negotiations far away in Europe.

Many British officers felt that Prevost had brought disgrace on the army. They had complained about his leadership before the ill-fated invasion, and now their criticisms increased. They maintained that their troops could easily have captured Plattsburgh even without Downie's fleet. The army would have had to withdraw, but it could have done so after a victory instead of appearing to flee from a defeat.

The British government recalled Prevost in March 1815 to answer this and other complaints. They accepted his explanation that he had no choice but to retreat since American control of the lake would have made it impossible for his army to maintain its communications and supply line. This explanation left some questions unanswered — why had he not tried to capture Platts- burgh before the eleventh? Why had he not acted at the same time as Downie? And the matter did not end there. A naval court seemed to criticize his conduct, and Prevost asked for an army court martial. He died, however, before it was held.

Throughout the war Prevost followed a defensive strategy. This was necessary in 1812 and 1813 when he had few troops and Britain could not send many. As well, he was following orders from London. As governor, Prevost was responsible for the se- curity of all British North America and could not afford to take the risks that lower-level commanders like Brock or Harvey could take. But by 1814 conditions were changing. Britain could send large numbers of troops under good commanders, all of them with combat experience. More supplies and money were avail-

The American fleet of Captain Thomas MacDonough defeats the
British squadron of Captain George Downie in Plattsburgh Bay,
September, 1814.
[Courtesy of National Archives of Canada, C41207.]

able and the Royal Navy was putting severe pressure on the
United States seaboard. These changed conditions justified a
different strategy, but Prevost continued as before. When he invaded the United States, he had a definite superiority in troops
and probably could have captured Plattsburgh using only the
army. In Yeo's opinion, if Prevost had seized the American position, their ships would have been forced to sail out of the bay and
onto the lake. The British ships would then have had the advantage because of their longer range guns.

Prevost's retreat from Plattsburgh ended the fighting along
the Lower Canadian frontier.

There was one final land battle, the Battle of New Orleans, in
January 1815. By the time it was fought, the two countries were
making peace in Europe, but there was no way for the British
government to call it off. Thus, Major General Edward Paken-
ham was killed and his army suffered heavy losses in a battle
which made no difference to the outcome of the war or to the
terms of the peace treaty. This American victory did, however,
greatly affect the career of the American commander. Andrew
Jackson gained so much fame from it that it helped him win

election as president in 1828. As well, Americans regard this as the last battle of the war and a great victory for their side. It is one reason for their pride in their country's record of the War of 1812.

ATLANTIC COAST

Throughout 1814, the American coast continued to suffer from the tight British naval blockade. The pressure increased in April when the blockade was extended to New England by Vice Admiral Alexander Cochrane, who had taken over command from Admiral Warren. Cochrane had many years' experience in naval warfare and was more aggressive than Warren had been. On April 7, British sailors raided up the Connecticut River and destroyed American ships there. This was only the beginning of more serious raids, some of which led to the conquest of American territory.

Communications overland between New Brunswick and Quebec were difficult because Maine extended so far north. When troops were ordered to march to Quebec in the winter — because the St. Lawrence was frozen — they were forced to take a long, roundabout route. With the objective of establishing a straighter and shorter line of communication on British territory, Sherbrooke was directed to occupy as much of Maine as necessary. His first move, in July, was to send an expedition to capture Moose Island in Passamaquoddy Bay, just across the boundary from New Brunswick. This was accomplished easily and the British troops went on to take the towns of Castine, Bangor and Machias, all without any resistance from the Americans.

By September 15, the eastern corner of Maine was in British control with a British military governor and a garrison at Castine. The people willingly took an oath not to resist. They preferred a quiet life and profitable trade with New Brunswick and Nova Scotia.

Seapower transporting regulars from Europe made possible the British success in Maine. It also enabled the British to carry out major raids which were not intended to conquer territory, but rather to threaten American cities in order to draw American attention away from the war against Canada. However, Prevost also wanted them to inflict destruction in retaliation for Ameri-

Battle of New Orleans. Centre in the foreground is
Major General Andrew Jackson, hero of this battle.
[Courtesy of the Buffalo and Erie County Historical Society.]

can raids against settlements in Upper Canada. Of course, these
raids would also have the effect of increasing pressure on the
United States to end the war.

The first British target was the United States capital, Washington, D.C. In July, President Madison had put General William
Winder in charge of the capital's defences. Earlier, in the Niagara
Peninsula, Winder had shown himself to be a poor leader, but he
had the advantage of being related to the governor of Maryland.
This appointment so annoyed Armstrong that he took no active
role in developing defences but left everything to Winder, with
the result that no one prepared gun positions or other strong
defences. Once again, the incompetence of American leaders
made things easy for British commanders.

On August 19, an army under Major General Robert Ross
landed and headed north along the Patuxent River. They had
no trouble as they marched along good roads under shady trees.
The Americans blew up their own gunboats in the river and the
sailors headed for Washington to help defend it. A few regulars
were collected, as were thousands of militiamen. But without
clear directions, most of them simply stood about on a ridge
overlooking a small river. On the other side was the village of
Bladensburg on the road the British would have to take to

Washington. When they were ready, the British fired rockets and attacked boldly across the bridge, whereupon, the defenders almost immediately bolted. This battle has been called the "Bladensburg Races" because the defending army and the American government ran away so quickly. Only the seamen from the gunboats stood and fought hard until they were overwhelmed by the larger British force.

The British burned several public buildings in Washington, including the president's home. Only the exterior walls survived, and when it was later rebuilt, they were whitewashed to cover the marks of the fire. This is why it is called the White House. Americans and some people in Britain criticized this destruction in Washington while others, such as Reverend John Strachan, argued that it was justified because of what the Americans had done to York.

Ross's army returned to its ships, which then moved up Chesapeake Bay to Baltimore. The troops landed on September 12, but the American defenders fought more bravely than they had at Washington. They were also better prepared. For example, ships had been sunk in the harbour to prevent British warships from getting close enough to do serious damage. The British nonetheless used guns and rockets to bombard the city on the night of September 13. (During this bombardment, Frances Scott Key, a Baltimore lawyer, wrote the words of what is now the American national anthem). After this, the British commanders decided they had accomplished what they wanted and that it was not worth heavy losses to try to capture the city. By the fifteenth, the army was back on its ships and in a few days these left Chesapeake Bay.

These British attacks shook American morale. The fact that the government could not even protect its own capital seemed clear proof of weak and incompetent leadership at the top. As a result, Armstrong left his position as Secretary of War, but it is not clear if he quit or was fired. This vital post was left unfilled for almost a month until President Madison appointed James Monroe, who was also Secretary of State. It was several weeks before the government began to function again in Washington. By then, the war was as good as ended.

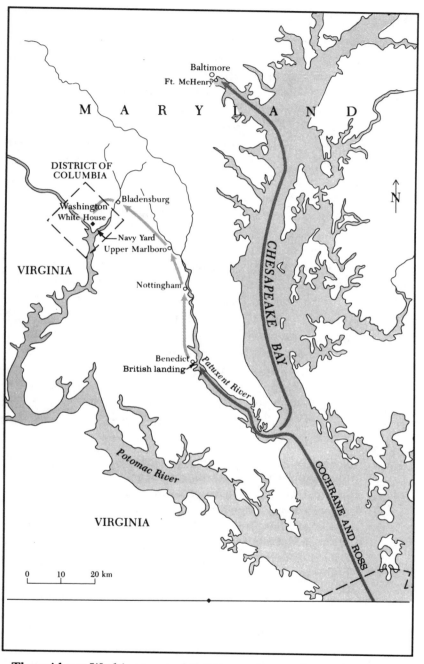

The raids on Washington and Baltimore, August-September, 1814.
[*Adapted from* The War of 1812: Land Operations, *by George F. G. Stanley
(Toronto, Macmillan of Canada, 1983), p. 339.*]

THE CANADIAN PEOPLE

The problems and strains of the war continued during 1814. The people of western Upper Canada and the Niagara Peninsula suffered raids and invasion that other areas did not experience. Yet nowhere in the province could people live normal lives.

Drummond repealed martial law in January but soon found that farmers around Kingston would not sell supplies to the government. In April he imposed it again to force them to do so. He also requested more money to retire government debts, pay wages and purchase supplies. As these measures did not overcome the problem of insufficient food, Drummond forbade the use of grain to make whisky and the export of most farm produce.

The shortage of food was greatest in the Niagara Peninsula and western Upper Canada because of the destruction caused by the fighting there and the large number of troops, Indians and militia who had to be fed. Moreover, American raids west of the Grand River destroyed virtually all of that area's resources. A man who was living near Port Talbot during the American raid in August gave his account of it many years later. The raiders, he said, took everything they were able to remove. "What they could not take with them ... they committed to the flames or otherwise destroyed. The grist mill which Colonel Talbot had erected, and which had proved very serviceable to the infant settlement, was totally destroyed."[4]

There are no reports that anyone starved to death, but certainly times were hard for ordinary people. Homes and barns, livestock and crops, mills, businesses of various kinds and even furniture and clothing were lost. Jacob Wood of Oxford County, for example, had his house, furniture, barn, hay, grain and carpentry shop and tools destroyed. He was given $200 by the Loyal and Patriotic Society. Henry Lestor "lost his grain, fences, and potatoes"; he was given $50.[5]

The government continued its efforts to catch and punish traitors. The Assembly agreed, at Drummond's request, to strengthen the laws against treason, including among other changes, the authority to seize the property of traitors. At least seventy people from the western and Niagara areas were charged with treason but most had fled to the United States. Still, several treason trials were held, the largest being at Ancaster in May and

Military rites: the reburial of American soldiers from Fort Erie.
[Courtesy of Richard W. Roeller.]

June, 1814. Here nineteen men were tried in Rousseau's Union Hotel because it was the largest building in town. Among the men found guilty were Aaron Stevens who had been employed by the government in the Indian Department but who confessed that he had spied for the Americans; Samuel and Stephen Hartwell who had joined Hull when he invaded in 1812 and who had tried to capture loyal citizens; Isaiah (or Jonah) Brink who had joined American raiding parties as had Benjamin Simmons (or Simmonds).[6] Although fifteen defendants were convicted and sentenced to hang, only eight were actually executed. The others were reprieved but given prison sentences. One later escaped, three died in prison of disease, and the rest were pardoned on condition they leave Upper Canada and never return.

Clearly, 1814 was the most difficult year for both government and people. The trials and executions of traitors showed that the government was determined to act firmly against any threat from within the province.

The Assembly also approved stronger measures to defend Upper Canada. It voted more money to improve roads for military use and amended the militia law so that the government could organize battalions of incorporated militia and keep them in service up to a year. This meant a heavier demand on the manpower of the province and more money for their training. All these developments indicated a hardening of the people's will

111

to continue to fight. This is one way in which a sense of nationalism begins: resistance to an external enemy.

The problems of treason and invasion did not trouble Lower Canada or the Maritime colonies. The main changes people there saw were increased numbers of soldiers and sailors and more government spending. For a time, merchants of Nova Scotia and New Brunswick were not allowed to trade with their American neighbours. Their businesses suffered, but when the British occupied eastern Maine they were able to renew their trade with the Americans. The New Brunswick assembly asked for a change in the boundary with Maine, but a final decision on that — as on other matters — depended upon the peace negotiations in Europe.

5
OUT OF WAR TO A LONG PEACE

S WITH THE START of the War of 1812, so with its ending, much depended upon decisions and events in Europe. While Napoleon was being defeated, both the Americans and the British had to consider how much Britain could increase her forces in North America. To Madison and his cabinet, stronger British forces meant invasion and possible defeat of United States armies. To the British prime minister, Lord Liverpool, stronger forces meant security for Canada plus the possibility of a peace settlement favourable mainly to Britain.

But Liverpool could not simply send all his troops and ships to North America. Many countries were involved in the negotiations which followed Napoleon's defeat. It took a long time for them to agree on a peace settlement. For a while, late in 1814 and early in 1815, there was even a possibility of fighting among the allies, and some British troops had to be kept available. Thus Wellington had to stay in Europe with part of his army, and the British government had to devote a good deal of attention to problems there. As well, some warships had to be kept in home waters to defend British merchant vessels from venturesome American privateers.

The government also had to consider the mood of the British people. For over twenty years they had endured the burdens of fighting against France. Continued war against the United States could soon become very unpopular.

The situation in Europe had a major bearing on British-American peace negotiations.

A LONG AND DELICATE PROCESS

During the negotiations each side had to recognize what was vital to the other and, therefore, what could be demanded. Both sides wanted not only to end the war, but to make a peace that would last. This further complicated negotiations, and many issues were left unsettled when the peace treaty was finally signed.

As conditions changed in Europe and North America, the delegates of each side had to consult their governments. The American representatives were required to send messages to Madison and wait for replies, a very slow process in the days of sailing vessels. It is easy to see why the negotiations took up most of 1814. At first, the American government made severe demands on Britain in return for peace. This may be seen in the government's instructions to its delegates in January 1814. Harking back to the reasons that the President had stated in 1812 for going to war, the delegates were to insist that the British end impressment from American ships and the blockade of the Atlantic coast. They were to press Britain to accept United States naval dominance of the lakes, to pay for American losses resulting from the blockade as well as from raids along the coast and, even, to hand over Canada to the United States. These instructions remained their guide until June. It then became clear that Britain would not agree to such harsh terms, and Madison's government began to soften its demands. For example, by the time formal talks began in August, the United States had dropped any reference to the causes of the war.

Initially, the British made tough demands also. One was for the creation of an Indian nation south and west of Lake Erie. The British proposed that the boundaries of such a nation be permanent, meaning that American settlers could not cross them. But there were already about a hundred thousand Americans pioneering beyond the suggested boundary line. This demand was rejected by the American delegates.

114

The other main British proposals were equally unacceptable to the Americans. They included a change in the boundary line between the United States and British North America, an end to American rights to fish off the east coast of British North America and to dry fish on the shores, and the removal of American naval forces and fortifications on the Great Lakes.

Eventually both sides recognized that the only way they would reach agreement was by moderating their demands. By September, the British had dropped the insistence on an Indian nation but still asked that the Indian position be restored to what it had been before the war. The Americans took until October to agree.

The British continued to insist on their proposed boundary changes, which would have given Canada part of Maine, a strip along the east side of the Niagara River and Michilimackinac Island. In fact, the British already held eastern Maine and Fort Niagara, and with the help of their Indian allies they controlled the vast territory west and south of Michilimackinac. The American government and its delegates were nonetheless unanimous in their refusal to give up any American land. Then the victory at Plattsburg strengthened their determination. The deadlock on this issue was ended by the British because of the sudden danger of war in Europe and the advice given by the Duke of Wellington.

Wellington was asked by the government to take over command in North America. He refused, explaining that without superiority on the Great Lakes, changing the commander or sending more troops would make no difference. As long as the Americans controlled Lakes Champlain and Erie and had a fleet on Lake Ontario, they could invade Canada and threaten any British army invading the United States. Wellington went on in his letter, "...it is my opinion that the war has been a most successful one and highly honourable to the British arms; but from particular circumstances, such as the want of naval superiority on the Lakes, you have not been able to carry it into the enemy's territory...."[1] After pointing out that the Americans still held parts of Canada, he argued that the British could not insist on the United States giving up territory unless they were prepared to surrender Canadian territory. The government, he suggested, might as well make peace "now."

Downie's defeat on Lake Champlain and Prevost's retreat were events that supported the Duke's argument. But for the

British to gain total control of Lakes Champlain, Ontario and Erie would have required a tremendous expenditure of money and effort — without any guarantee of success. The British failure at Plattsburg was thus an important reason why Liverpool softened British demands.

The British delegates stopped insisting that the Americans give up territory. With that obstacle removed, the two sides soon agreed on a treaty. The Treaty of Ghent was signed on December 24, 1814. When the news reached the United States in February, people rejoiced. In contrast to the vote for war, which had divided the Senate, not a single senator voted against the peace treaty. The people of British North America, however, were not as happy with the terms that had been agreed upon.

The Treaty of Ghent ended the war and obliged each side to return what it had conquered. That was about all it actually settled. There was to be no independent Indian nation and nothing was said about impressment, blockade or fisheries. Commissions were set up to decide the boundary question.

Yet the treaty was very important. It began a new kind of relationship between the United States and Britain, one in which they settled their disagreements by negotiation rather than by war. Never again did the United States make war on Canada. Later, after Canada became independent, it negotiated for itself with the United States. The two countries have had their differences and still have, including disagreements over fisheries, but ever since the Treaty of Ghent they have managed to settle problems peacefully.

THE TREATY OF GHENT AND THE INDIANS

The people who had the most to gain or lose were the Indians south and west of the Great Lakes. The British had proposed that they be a party to the peace treaty, but the Americans refused. Thus the Indians had no one to speak for them at Ghent.

After the signing of the treaty, the Americans were eager for the British to get their troops out of Prairie du Chien and Michilimackinac so that the Indians would not hope for outside support against the United States government. The British withdrew first from Prairie du Chien and finally, in July, from Michilimackinac. The Americans then pulled out of Malden.

View of Buffalo Harbor, 1825. This frontier town, fully
recovered from its destruction during the war, was on the
threshold of its first major boom with the completion
of the Erie Canal to nearby Tonawanda.
[Courtesy of the Buffalo and Erie County Historical Society.]

The Indians had been preparing to continue fighting, but
most gave this up when the British withdrew. Representatives of
the tribes in the old northwest began negotiating with the United
States. Treaties meant to restore Indian-American relations to
what they had been in 1811 were signed. But neither side could
go back in time. Thousands more American pioneers were
pushing westward into territory which the Indians regarded as
their own. The Indians would continue to resist but much more
weakly than before 1812; and they no longer had a European ally
to help them.

In April 1816 the United States Congress passed a law forbidding trade between Indians within American territory and
foreign traders. This meant the end of contacts between Canadian traders and Indians beyond the United States border. From
then on, if Indians wanted manufactured goods they would have
to get them from Americans. If they had furs to sell they would
have to deal with American traders. This development marked
the end of a fur trade between Canadians and Indians south and
west of the Lakes that went back almost two hundred years. Such

a change would have come about eventually, but the War of 1812 hastened it.

The Indians in Canada continued to live peacefully on the lands they had held before the war. Their loyalty and important contributions to Canada's defence were remembered, and many Indians still take pride in their ancestors' bravery during the War of 1812.

DISARMAMENT ON THE LAKES

The shipbuilding contest on Lake Ontario had become a very large, expensive and dangerous competition by the end of 1814. The two new ships started at Kingston that year were to be even more powerful than the Royal Navy's ocean-going vessels. The two big ships the Americans started would have been as powerful and even larger. They would have been the biggest warships in the world if they had been completed!

There were other plans both for shipbuilding and the development of naval bases. Dr. Dunlop wrote graphically about one proposal made at the end of 1814 and its consequences:

> ...it was proposed to build a large ship on Lake Huron
> ... that would be able, from her size, and the weight of
> her metal, to cope with the small vessels that com-
> posed the American flotilla on Lake Erie. As there is
> a channel through Lake Saint Clair, and the Rivers
> Detroit and Saint Clair, by which she could pass from
> one lake into the other, an inlet, called Penetangui-
> shene, was selected as the proper site of a new dock-
> yard, and a better site could hardly have been selected
> ... it was a narrow-mouthed, deep bay, with plenty of
> water for any size of craft, and a fine bold shore, easily
> defensible against any ships that could approach; but
> unluckily, Penetanguishene was in the woods, thirty
> miles from Lake Simcoe; and before a ship of the line
> could be built, a road must be cut, and stones broke
> along it.
> ... in the early part of December, I volunteered my
> services, and, as nobody else envied the job, they were
> accepted; and a company of the Canadian Fencibles,
> with about the same number of militia, under the di-
> rection of Colonel Cockburn of the Quarter Master

General's Department, was despatched up to the north, with instructions to have the road cut at all hazards.

Things went on pretty much the same till we had nearly completed our business; no labour had been spared in perfecting our work. Bridges had been thrown across streams in the depth of winter, when officers and men had to stand for hours up to the middle in ice-cold water; ravines had to be bridged when the logs had to be dragged out of swamps through four feet of snow. The month of March was far advanced when we promised ourselves a pleasant summer in the comfortable quarters that we meant to build for ourselves at Penetanguishene, when all our anticipations were set aside by the arrival of the appalling intelligence that peace had been concluded between his Majesty and the United States. This showed half pay staring us in the face; however, soldiers have nothing to do but obey — we were withdrawn — all the expenditure incurred went for nothing; we were marched to Toronto (then York,) and sent to join our respective regiments."[2]

It did not make sense in peacetime to try to keep up the tremendous pace of shipbuilding. The Americans suggested that both sides reduce their naval forces on the lakes to a minimum. In effect, neither side would maintain a navy there, only a few armed vessels to deal with smugglers or other lawbreakers. They argued that the best security for both Canada and the United States was to have no means of attacking each other on the lakes.

The British agreed to the American suggestion and negotiations followed during 1816. The treaty, reached in April 1817, is known as the Rush-Bagot Agreement after the men who signed it: Richard Rush, American acting Secretary of State, and Charles Bagot, British minister to Washington. The two countries agreed to have only two armed vessels on the lakes above Niagara Falls, one on Lake Ontario and one on Lake Champlain. These would be small vessels, each armed with one cannon. Immediately, both sides reduced their fleets.

Most of the British ships on Lake Ontario survived until the 1830s when they were either sold or sunk in the lake near Kingston. The United States vessels also were left to decay. The Rush-

Bagot Agreement is still in force and undoubtedly has prevented clashes between Canada and the United States which might have led to wider conflicts.

Despite disarmament, each side was concerned about security in case of another war. For example, the American Secretary of War, James Monroe, in February, 1815, prepared a plan for an attack on Canada which would avoid the mistakes of the previous three years. His idea was to leave only militia on the Niagara and Detroit frontiers, while concentrating all the regulars that could be collected, along with about 30,000 militia, against the St. Lawrence between Montreal and Kingston. The dynamic Major General Brown would be in full command of the campaign. This very sensible plan from the American point of view put the emphasis where it should have gone from the beginning of the conflict.

For some years after the peace, military roads were constructed, one running east from Sackets Harbor and one west from Plattsburg. However, forts were not kept up and Brown's idea of a fort on the American bank of the St. Lawrence (which could have seriously threatened movement up the river) was never put into effect.

On the Canadian side, the authorities continued to worry about security. One measure they took was to establish a naval base at Penetanguishene in 1818. Another was the building of the Rideau Canal, at a total cost of over a million pounds, the biggest and most expensive military work which the British government undertook in all of British North America. A third was fortifications at Kingston where the first Fort Henry was erected by 1820. It was later demolished and the present Fort Henry was finished 28 years after the end of the war. The naval dockyard at Kingston lasted for several decades.

BOUNDARIES

Both sides were dissatisfied with parts of the boundary between British North America and the United States. Three commissions, each consisting of an American and a British member, were set up in 1816 to try to settle all these problems. They reached agreement on most issues, and this helped to reduce the potential for future conflict.

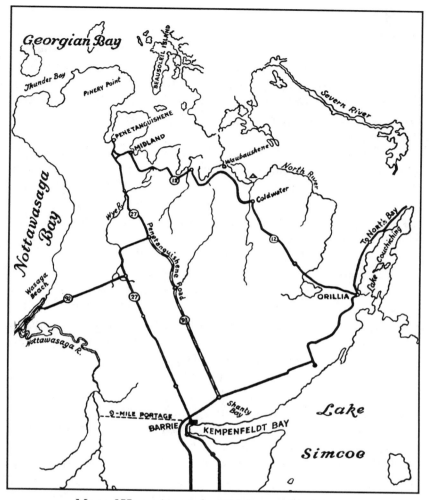

Map of Huronia; modern highways are shown.
[Adapted from The Establishments at Penetanguishene:
Bastion of the North 1814-1856, *by E.M. Jury (London, Ontario:
The University of Western Ontario, Museum of Indian Archaeology,
Bulletin No. 12, 1959), p. 55.]*

The first line agreed upon was from the St. Lawrence to the western end of Lake Superior. Some of the major islands were given to the United States, others to Canada. This settled the boundary between the most heavily populated parts of the two countries, where problems were most likely to occur. The same commission could not agree on the boundary from Lake Superior to Lake of the Woods. That was not finally settled until the Webster-Ashburton Treaty of 1842.

The boundary along the 49th parallel from Lake of the Woods to the Rocky Mountains was quickly decided, but the two sides disagreed on the line from the Rockies to the Pacific Ocean. They decided on joint occupation for ten years and, finally, an 1846 treaty established the 49th parallel as the boundary for this area as well. There was much argument about the boundary in Passamaquoddy Bay and between Maine, New Brunswick and Lower Canada.

The British insisted on keeping Grand Manan Island, and in 1817 the Americans agreed in return for several other islands in the Bay. The boundary along the St. Croix River was not in dispute, but from its source to the St. Lawrence, each side had very different views. The Webster-Ashburton Treaty eventually decided this boundary.

The Treaty of Ghent had also left the fisheries issue for later negotiations, but before these were undertaken, trouble occurred along the east coast. British warships seized American vessels fishing within the coastal limits of British North America. For a while there was a danger that the Americans would respond with force. Realizing that to exclude American fishing vessels from these waters would require a large fleet and great expense, the British offered to compromise. The Americans accepted. In their turn, they recognized that they were unlikely to obtain everything they wanted without fighting Britain.

Negotiations proceeded slowly until 1818. In the agreement of that year, the Americans received the right to fish along the western and southern coasts of Newfoundland, around the Magdalen Islands, and along the Labrador coast. They could enter any bay to obtain wood and water, to shelter from a storm or to repair damage.

The solution was not perfect, and there have since been many disputes between Canada and the United States over east coast fisheries. But the agreement of 1818 was a very important step towards the peaceful settlement of the problem.

PEACE

By the 1820s, Britain and the United States had created a strong foundation for lasting peace between them. Much of the fear of renewed war had faded, and problems that could have caused armed clashes had been resolved. The war provided a lesson which the British and American governments appear to have learned: war between them would cause a great deal of death and destruction and neither side would win a total victory.

In the United States, the end of the conflict and the drawing of definite boundaries opened the way for massive population growth and territorial expansion. Roads, canals and soon railways were being built. New towns and industries sprang up. Americans felt their country was strong, truly independent and important. What Albert Gallatin, one of the American negotiators at Ghent, wrote in 1816 was indeed happening:

> The war has been productive of evil and of good, but I think the good preponderates ... The war has re-newed and reinstated the national feelings and char-acter which the Revolution had given, and which were daily lessening. The people have now more general objects of attachment, with which their pride and political opinions are connected. They are more Americans; they feel and act more as a nation, and I hope that the permanency of the Union is thereby better secured. [3]

THE LIFE OF THE PEOPLE

The lives of most Canadians were affected by the war though not always to their detriment. When the war started, prices of goods and services rose. This benefited farmers who could grow more crops or who had horses and wagons for hire, as well as mer-chants who imported, shipped and sold goods. Skilled workers received higher wages. But farmers who were unable to grow more, and many people living in towns, experienced harder times because their living costs rose. People whose homes or farms were destroyed and the families of militiamen who had been killed or wounded suffered as well.

Shortages of food and high prices were caused partly by the need to feed more soldiers and sailors, by the absence of mili-tiamen from their farms, and by the destruction of houses, barns and mills in Upper Canada. The end of the war removed these causes, but reconstruction of farms and businesses would take several years. An American travelling from the Niagara River to

Reinternment of soldiers, Lundy's Lane Methodist Church,
c. 1900.
[Courtesy of the Archives of Ontario, S9092-6355.]

Detroit in 1816 wrote, "I was most sensibly struck with the dev-astation which had been made by the late war, [farms] formerly in high cultivation, now laid waste; houses entirely evacuated and forsaken; provisions of all kinds very scarce; and, where peace and plenty abounded, poverty and destruction now stalked over the land."[4]

To add to the woes of the people, food shortages were ag-gravated by poor harvests resulting from bad weather in 1812, 1814 and for several years after the war.

Food and lumber came into Canada before 1812 from northern New York and northern Vermont. Some of the prod-ucts were exported down the St. Lawrence to Britain. During the war, these supplies continued to be imported and were very im-portant to the British forces as well as to the civilian population. Such trade was illegal in war time, but the American government was unable to stop it. The trade continued after the war, but as Upper Canadian farms were restored, as immigrants came in and began farming, and as British troops were withdrawn, depend-ence on American food supplies decreased. By the 1820s Upper Canadian farmers were even selling their produce to Lower Canada, where agriculture was less productive. Soon Upper Canada would become a big exporter of wheat, much of it to the British market.

The war increased employment for both skilled and unskilled workers. They found jobs building ships, forts, barracks and roads as well as transporting men and supplies. Wages for militiamen became another source of income for some families. There were poor people in Canada before the war, however, and postwar prosperity did not eliminate the problem of poverty.

Until 1817, the Loyal and Patriotic Society continued to give money to help the families of militiamen killed or wounded during the war. The small amount of money left after that year was given to a society that helped poor people. In 1819 a contribution of £4,000 arrived from England. The Society decided to use the money to found a hospital at York, which later became the Toronto General Hospital.

By stimulating trade up the St. Lawrence-Great Lakes route, the War of 1812 became one of the factors which led to later canal-building. Trade continued to grow after 1814. Food, lumber and furs went downriver and manufactured goods came upriver. But Upper Canada's export trade, especially in bulky foodstuffs, was restricted because of the high costs of this route. Upper Canadians were joined by Montreal businessmen in proposing canals as the answer to the problem. By 1824 the Lachine Canal had opened and construction of the Welland Canal was underway.

One lasting effect of the war was on immigration. American pioneers had been important in settling Upper Canada ever since the end of the American Revolution. That immigration stopped in 1812. Even after the war, the British government, remembering the problems of disloyalty, did not want Americans to come to Upper Canada. The government, therefore, adopted a two-part policy.

First, it tried to discourage American immigrants by instructing the lieutenant governor not to grant them land or administer the oath of allegiance. Opposition came from large landowners who wanted to sell land to Americans and from residents who had come earlier from the United States and who now feared they would lose their right to vote, hold office and perhaps even to own land. The quarrel over this issue created much political turmoil for several years.

Next, the government sought to populate Upper Canada with people whose loyalty could be relied on. A number of British regiments were disbanded in Upper Canada and the men were given land. Emigration from Britain was encouraged and financed. As a result, parts of Upper Canada were settled sooner than they might otherwise have been.

Soldiers were encouraged to settle in Nova Scotia and New Brunswick as well. From 1813 to 1816, nearly two thousand blacks were also settled in these colonies. They were slaves who had fled to freedom on British ships raiding the American coast.

These small groups, settled with government help, hinted at what was to come. About 600,000 people from the British Isles would emigrate to British North America between 1815 and 1841. Peace in North America was an important cause of this massive movement.

OTHER LEGACIES

Many reminders of the War of 1812 still exist — forts along the border, weapons and uniforms in museums, the *Nancy* at Wasaga Beach, the *Hamilton* and *Scourge* in Lake Ontario, Perry's *Niagara* at Erie. Another legacy is people's memories, for there are Canadians who have not forgotten that their ancestors fought in the war.

Reaction to the war strongly affected the society and politics of Upper Canada for many years after 1814. Anti-American feelings increased and were combined with a greater sense of patriotism or British-Canadian "nationalism." These legacies have faded but not disappeared entirely from Canada.

The fear of American immigrants soon passed. Ties of trade, family and even friendship across the border continued or were created. Yet many Upper Canadians, and particularly the leaders of society and government, disliked what the United States represented. It stood for republicanism and democracy in contrast to their own values of monarchy, an established church and an ordered (or class) society. They believed that American political principles and social practices produced lawlessness and disorder, and undermined religion and morality.

The men who had been the leaders of Upper Canada during the war (Reverend John Strachan, William Allan, John Beverley Robinson, Christopher Hagerman) believed they should continue to lead afterwards. They became known as the Family

The coat of Sir Isaac Brock, containing the fatal bullet-hole.
[Courtesy of the Archives of Ontario, S1427.]

Compact, and one of the ties among them was that of proven loyalty during 1812-14. The War, therefore, provided one basis for the rule of the province by a small group. It also enabled the Compact to attack their opponents with the very powerful charge of being disloyal. They denounced reformers' demands for

Chippawa: scene of the battle.
[Courtesy of the Archives of Ontario, S9092-6355.]

changes in the system of government, land-granting and education as being pro-American — which automatically made them dangerous.

On the other hand, there was a sense of patriotism which was shared by reformers and supporters of the Compact. People felt they were Canadians but at the same time part of a greater whole, the British Empire. They had fought in the militia or other forces to defend their homes, but this had also been defence of the Empire. They could glorify Brock, a British general, and make him a Canadian hero. In part, this was because flank companies of the militia had fought under him and he had praised them. Events such as these strengthened belief in the militia myth.

Many people also emphasized the role of the Canadian heroine, Laura Secord, and heroes like Billy Green and Salaberry. Lately, Canadians have come to a greater awareness of the Indian contribution and recognize men like Tecumseh and Norton as courageous and important leaders.

In the Maritimes, merchants and others criticized British concessions to the Americans on the New Brunswick boundary and the fisheries. Yet the sense of being loyal British subjects remained strong throughout this region. As well, Maritimers may

Archaeologists investigating the Fort Erie excavation believed
to be American soldiers from the War of 1812.
[Photo by Leonard Le Page, courtesy of The Standard, *St. Catharines.]*

have felt a kinship with distant Upper Canada because they had
sent soldiers, supplies and money to help its defence against a
common enemy.

Anti-American and pro-British attitudes in Lower Canada
were strengthened by the war, although naturally there was not
the same feeling of kinship with Britain because of differences in
language, law and religion. French Canadians appreciated Britain's role, but, above all, they glorified their own part in the war,
particularly at the battle of Chateauguay. A sense of French Canadian nationalism had existed before 1812 and the war en-
hanced it. At this period, nationalism was not directed towards
breaking away from British rule.

WHO WON THE WAR?

There is one final question: who won the war? The answer de-
pends almost entirely on what country you live in.

The Americans tend to think they did. They won several big
land battles that in certain cases prevented major British inva-

sions. They conquered part of Upper Canada and won control of two lakes. They still take great pride in several single-ship victories. Combat at sea and on land created heroes and inspired traditions in the navy and army. For instance, the grey dress uniform worn by the cadets at the United States Military Academy at West Point commemorates the victory at Chippawa (1814) where the troops wore gray. Finally, the United States did not lose anything. In fact, Americans believed that their country was more respected as a result of the war, that it had proved its strength and independence.

The Canadian view is different. Canadians believe the main American aim was to conquer Canada. This was not achieved, and therefore the Canadian side won the war. Certainly, the major American war effort was on land and was directed against Canada, particularly Upper Canada. Canadians remember the defeat of large American forces by smaller numbers of defenders. They forget or disregard western Upper Canada or American victories on Lakes Erie and Champlain as well as in single-ship fighting at sea. Canada did not have war aims because it did not seek war. Simply, the fact that Canada survived is an argument that the defenders won.

There was a group who clearly lost as a result of this war: native peoples south and west of Lake Erie. The death of Tecumseh took the heart out of much of the western Indians' resistance to United States expansion. The peace negotiations offered them some hope but the expectation of a separate Indian nation probably allied with Great Britain, was not realistic and Britain lacked the power to force such a settlement upon the United States. Probably the most decisive effects of the war were for the native peoples of the Great Lakes basin.

The War of 1812 received little attention in British history books because it was such a minor affair compared to the long and hard-fought Napoleonic Wars. Britain did not lose anything and was not forced to renounce its policies of impressment and blockade. But these were wartime policies which Britain did not need to use after 1814. The growth of British power, prestige and wealth during the nineteenth century pushed this little war far into the background. If there is a British point of view, it probably agrees with the Canadian one.

Any study of the War of 1812 shows that history is not simply the facts of what happened. It is a study of people's actions and beliefs combined with an attempt to understand and interpret them. History is about the how and why of the past. That is why it lives and, like all living things, changes.

NOTES

Introduction

1. J.C.A. Stagg, *Mr. Madison's War. Politics, Diplomacy, and Warfare in the Early American Republic, 1783-1830* (Princeton, NJ, 1983), p.162.

Chapter 1

1. 20 April, 1812, cited in N.K. Risjord, "1812: Conservatives, War Hawks and the Nation's Honor," *William and Mary Quarterly*, 3rd Series, XVIII (April, 1961), p. 205.
2. Cited in Stagg, p. 228-29. Benjamin F. Stickney, the American agent sent to Canada to examine its defences, presented his report in Februray, 1812.
3. Public Archives of Canada, C676, p. 217-18.
4. Cited in B. Perkins, (ed.), *The Causes of the War of 1812. National Honor or National Interest?* (New York, 1963), p. 116, 117.

Chapter 2

1. *War on the Detroit: the Chronicles of Thomas Vercheres de Boucherville and the Capitulation by an Ohio Volunteer.* Edited by M.M. Quaife (Chicago, 1940), p.81.
2. Public Archives of Canada, C676, 168-71.
3. Brock to Col. Baynes, York, 29 July 1812. E.A. Cruikshank (ed) *The Documentary History of the Campaign Upon the Niagara Frontier, 1812–1814* (Welland, Ont. 1896–1908), 9 vols., vol. 3, 153.
4. In F.B. Tupper, *The Life and Correspondence of Sir Isaac Brock, K.B.* (London, 1847), p. 262.
5. Brock to Lord Liverpool, 29 August. *Select British Documents of the Canadian War of 1812.* Edited by William Wood. (Toronto, 1920-1928), 3 vols., I, 508.
6. *Report of the Trial of Brigadier General Hull.* (New York, 1814), p.40. Evidence of Major Snelling. Stagg, 205 and n.133.

7. M. Smith, *A Geographical View of the British Possessions in North America*. (Baltimore, 1813), pp.88-89. On Smith himself, see *Dictionary of Canadian Biography* Frances G. Halpenny, gen. ed. (Toronto, 1983), vol. 5, 765-66.

8. Porter to Eustis, 30 August 1812 in E. A. Cruickshank (ed.), *The Documentary History of the Campaign upon the Niagara Frontier 1812-1814* (Welland, Ont. 1896-1908), 9 vols., vol.3, 1812, p.275.

9. William S. Dudley (ed.), *The Naval War of 1812, A Documentary History*. (Washington, D.C, 1985), vol.,1,166-70. The figures come from A. L. Burt, *The United States, Great Britain and British North America from the Revolution to the Establishment of Peace after the War of 1812* (New York, 1961), pp. 317-18 and George E. E. Nichols, "Notes on Nova Scotia Privateers," *Collections of the Nova Scotia Historical Society*, XIII (1908), 111-12, 131-52.

10. Cited in C. P. Stacey, "The War of 1812 in Canadian History," in *The Defended Border, Upper Canada and the War of 1812*. Edited by M. Zaslow (Toronto, 1964), p.334. Stacey assumed the speaker was Rev. John Strachan.

Chapter 3

1. Cited in J.M. Hitsman, *The Incredible War of 1812: A Military History* (Toronto 1965), 142.

2. W.S.MacNutt, *The Atlantic Provinces: The Emergence of a Colonial Society,1712-1857* (Toronto, 1965), 150; *Dictionary of National Biography*. Edited by Sir Leslie Stephen and Sir Sidney Lee (London, 1959-60), v.20, 603-04.

3. Cited by Charles Humphries in *The Defended Border*, 258.

4. Daniel A. Nelson, "Hamilton and Scourge: Ghost Ships of the War of 1812," *National Geographic*, vol. 163 (March, 1983), 289-313; Emily Cain, *Ghost Ships. Hamilton and Scourge: Historical Treasures from the War of 1812* (Toronto, 1983).

5. G.T. Altoff, "Oliver Hazard Perry and the Battle of Lake Erie," *The Michigan Historical Review*, 14 (Fall, 1988), 50.

6. Captain J. FitzGibbon to Captain William J. Kerr, 30 March, 1818 in E.A. Cruikshank (ed.), *The Documentary History*, vol. 6, 1813 (part 2), 120-21.

7. Cited in *Defended Border*, 81.

8. Merritt's Journal in *Select Documents* III, 607-08.

9. Major General Hall to Governor Tompkins, 30 December 1813 in *Documentary History*, vol.9, 68.

10. Cited in *Kingston Gazette*, 22 March, 1814, in *Documentary History*, vol.9, 234.

Chapter 4

1. Cited in G.F.G. Stanley, *The War of 1812, Land Operations* (Ottawa, 1983), 312.

2. Cited in *Select Documents*, III, 617.

3. William Dunlop, *Tiger Dunlop's Upper Canada*. Comprising Recollections of the American War of 1812-14 and Statistical Sketches of Upper Canada for the *Use of Emigrants*. By a Backwoodsman. Introduction by C.F. Klinck (Toronto, 1967), 54.

4. Edward Ermatinger, *Life of Colonel Talbot and the Talbot Settlement* (St. Thomas, Ont., 1859), 49; see also 52 and Drummond to Yeo, 13 November, 1814, in *Select Documents*, III, 290.

5. *The Report of the Loyal and Patriotic Society of Upper Canada* (Montreal, 1817), 209, 236.

6. W. R. Riddell, "The Ancaster 'Bloody Assize' of 1814," in *Defended Border*, 244-45.

Chapter 5

1. Wellington to Prime Minster, 9 November 1814, cited in Hitsman, 234-35.

2. Dunlop, *Tiger Dunlop's Upper Canada*, 56-7, 62.

3. Cited in Captain A.T. Mahan, *Sea Power in its Relations to the War of 1812*. (London, 1905, 2 vols.), II, 436.

4. Cited in *Defended Border*, 240.

CHRONOLOGY

1806

November–
December

Napoleon's Berlin Decree

1807

October–
December

British Orders in Council; Napoleon's
Fontainbleu and Milan Decrees; United States
Embargo

1811

November 7

Battle of Tippecanoe

1812

April 21

Conditional repeal of Orders in Council

June 18

United States declares war on Great Britain

June 23

British government repeals Orders in Council

June 24

Napoleon invades Russia

July 12

Brigadier General William Hull invades Upper
Canada

July 17

Captain Charles Roberts captures
Michilimackinac

August 13

Major General Isaac Brock reaches Amherstburg

August 16

Brock's forces capture Detroit

August 20

U.S.S. *Constitution* captures H.M.S. *Guerriere*

October 13

Battle of Queenston Heights and Brock's death

October 18

U.S.S. *Wasp* captures H.M.S. *Frolic* but is captured
by H.M.S. *Poictiers*

October 19

Napoleon's army begins its retreat from Moscow

October 25

U.S.S. *Constitution* captures H.M.S. *Macedonian*

November 10	Commodore Isaac Chauncey gains control of Lake Ontario
November 20	Major General Henry Dearborn invades Lower Canada
November 28-30	Brigadier General Alexander Smyth attempts to invade across the Niagara River
December 18	French army leaves Russian territory
December 29	U.S.S. *Constitution* captures H.M.S. *Java*

1813

January 9	British declaration of war on the United States
January 22	Lieutenant Colonel Henry Procter defeats Brigadier General James Wilkinson in a surprise attack at Frenchtown
February 22	Lieutenant Colonel George Macdonell raids Ogdensburg
February 24	U.S.S. *Hornet* sinks H.M.S. *Peacock*
April 27	Major General Dearborn's forces capture York
May 1-9	Procter's unsuccessful siege of Fort Meigs
May 25-27	Dearborn's forces capture Fort George and British forces under Brigadier General John Vincent retreat ultimately to Burlington Heights
May 29	British forces raid Sackets Harbor
June 1	H.M.S. *Shannon* captures U.S.S. *Chesapeake*
June 6	Battle of Stoney Creek
June 22	Laura Secord's walk to Beaver Dam
June 24	Battle of Beaver Dam
July 26-28	Procter's forces fail to capture Fort Meigs
July 31	Americans again occupy York
	Captain Robert Barclay lifts blockade of Presque Isle
August 1-4	Captain Oliver Perry takes his fleet out of Presque Isle
August 2	Procter's forces fail to take Fort Stephenson
August 8	During the night, U.S.S. *Hamilton* and *Scourge* sink in Lake Ontario off Twelve Mile Creek
September 3	U.S.S. *Enterprise* captures H.M.S. *Boxer*
September 10	Battle of Lake Erie, Perry defeats Barclay

September 27	General Procter begins retreat from Fort Malden
October 5	Battle of the Thames (Moraviantown) and death of Tecumseh
October 16-19	Battle of the Nations (Leipzig), Napoleon defeated in Germany
October 25	Battle of Chateauguay
November	British forces under Wellington invade France
November 11	Battle of Crysler's Farm
December 10	Brigadier-General George McClure's forces burn Newark and retreat to Fort Niagara
December 19	British capture Fort Niagara and burn Lewiston
December 29	British forces burn Black Rock and Buffalo

1814

January	Russian and allied troops invade France; American delegates sail for Europe to open peace negotiations
March 21	U.S.S. *Essex* is destroyed at anchorage off Valparaiso, Chile, by two British vessels
March 30	Wilkinson is defeated at Lacolle
March 31	The allies capture Paris
April 11	Napoleon abdicates
April 29	U.S.S. *Peacock* captures H.M.S. *Epervier*
May 6	British forces raid Oswego
	American forces capture Prairie du Chien and the British recapture it on July 20
May 23-June 21	Treason trials at Ancaster
June 2-5	William Clark, Governor of Missouri Territory, takes possession of Prairie du Chien and begins to build Fort Shelby
July 3	Major-General Jacob Brown invades Upper Canada and captures Fort Erie
July 5	Battle of Chippawa
July 11	British invade Maine
July 19	American troops burn St. David's
	British regain control of Prairie du Chien
July 21	Indians defeat an American force at Rock Island Rapids

July 25	Battle of Lundy's Lane
August 3	Lieutenant General Gordon Drummond begins siege of Fort Erie
August 4-5	Lieutenant Colonel George Croghan's attack on Michilimackinac fails
August 15	Drummond's assault on Fort Erie fails
August 19-25	British forces raid U.S. east coast, capture Washington and burn public buildings
September 1	British seize part of eastern Maine. Lieutenant General Sir George Prevost invades United States and reaches Plattsburgh on the 6th. U.S.S. *Wasp* sinks H.M.S. *Avon*
September 3-5	British forces capture U.S.S. *Tigress* and U.S.S. *Scorpion*
September 11	Captain Thomas Macdonough defeats British naval force in Plattsburgh Bay and Prevost orders his army to retreat.
September 12-15	British attack on Baltimore
September 17	Successful American sortie from Fort Erie against Drummond's batteries
November 5	American troops blow up Fort Erie and withdraw across the Niagara River
December 10	British troops land near mouth of Mississippi River
December 24	Treaty of Ghent signed

1815

January 8	Battle of New Orleans
March 23	U.S.S. *Hornet* captures H.M.S. *Penguin* in last naval action of the war

SELECTED FURTHER READING

Ballantyne, Lareine. *The Scout Who Led An Army*. Toronto: Macmillan, 1963. A novel about Billy Green.

Dudley, William S., ed. *The Naval War of 1812. A Documentary History*. Volume I:1812. Washington, D.C.: Naval Historical Center, Department of the Navy, 1985.

Dunlop, William. *Tiger Dunlop's Upper Canada*. Toronto: McClelland and Stewart, 1967.

Edmunds, R. D. *Tecumseh and the Quest for Indian Leadership*. Edited by O. Handlin. Boston: Little, Brown and Company, 1984.

Guitard, Michelle. *The Militia of the Battle of Chateauguay. A Social History*. Ottawa: National Historic Parks and Sites Branch, Parks Canada, Environment Canada, 1983.

Hayes, John F. *Treason at York*. Copp Clark, n.d. A novel of 1812-13 for young readers.

Hitsman, J. M. *The Incredible War of 1812: A Military History*. Toronto: University of Toronto Press, 1965.

McKenzie, Ruth. *Laura Secord: The Lady and the Legend*. Toronto: McClelland and Stewart, 1971.

Stanley, G.F.G. *The War of 1812: Land Operations*. Toronto: Macmillan of Canada, 1983. (Published in collaboration with National Museum of Man, National Museums of Canada.)

Sugden, John, *Tecumseh's Last Stand*. Norman: University of Oklahoma Press, 1985

Suthren, Victor. *Defend and Hold: The Batttle of Chateauguay*. Ottawa: Canadian War Museum, 1986

Zaslow, Morris, ed. *The Defended Border: Upper Canada and the War of 1812*. Toronto: Macmillan, 1964.

PRINCIPAL SOURCES ON THE HISTORY, DRESS AND ACCOUTREMENTS OF THE FIGHTING UNITS

Cattley, A. R. "The British Infantry Shako", *Journal of the Society for Army Historical Research* 15 (1936), 188-208.

Cruikshank, E. A. "Record of the Services of Canadian Regiments in the War of 1812", Canadian Military Institute, *Selected Papers from the Transactions of the Canadian Military Institute*. 1893-94, Part I; 1895-96, Part III; 1901, Part VII; 1902, Part VIII; 1903, Part IX; 1907, Part XI.

Darling, A. D. *Red Coat and Brown Bess*, Bloomfield, Ont.: Museum Restoration Service, Historical Arms Series, No. 12, 1970.

Guitard, Michelle (see above).

Irving, L. H. *Officers of the British Forces in Canada During the War of 1812*, Welland, Ont.: Tribune Print, 1908.

Katcher, P. R. N. and M. Youens. *The American War, 1812-1814*. Reading: Osprey Publishing, 1974.

Koke, R. J., "The Britons who fought on the Canadian Frontier. Uniforms of the War of 1812", *New York Historical Society Quarterly*, 45(1961), 141-94.

Rankin, R. H. *Military Headdress: A Pictorial History of Military Headgear from 1660 to 1914*. London: Arms and Armour Press, 1976.

"The Service of British Regiments in Canada and North America. A Resume with a chronological list of uniforms portrayed in sources consulted", compiled by Charles H. Stewart, Librarian, Ottawa, Department of National Defence Library, 1964.

Summers, J.L. and R. Chartrand. *Military Uniforms in Canada, 1665-1970*, Ottawa: Canadian War Museum, National Museum of Man, National Museums of Canada, Historical Publication No. 16, 1981.

INDEX

Page numbers in **boldface** indicate pictures.

OTHER DUNDURN TITLES RELATING TO THE WAR OF 1812

Armstrong, Frederick H. *Handbook of Upper Canadian Chronology*, 1985.

Fryer, Mary Beacock. *Battlefields of Canada*, 1986.

The Bibliography of Ontario History. Edited by Gaétan Gervais, et al., 1989.

Hall, Roger and Gordon Dodds. *Ontario: Two Hundred Years in Pictures*, 1990.

Patterns of the Past: Interpreting Ontario's History. Edited by Roger Hall, et al., 1988.

Old Ontario: Essays in Honour of J.M.S. Careless. Edited by David Keane and Colin Read, 1990.

MacKenzie, Ruth. *James FitzGibbon: Defender of Upper Canada*, 1983.

Scadding, Henry. *Toronto of Old*, 1987.

White, Randall. *Ontario 1610-1985: A Political and Economic History*, 1985.

Wohler, J. Patrick. *Charles de Salaberry: Soldier of the Empire, Defender of Quebec*, 1984.

For Younger Readers

Robinson, Helen Calster. *Laura: A Portrait of Laura Secord*, 1981.